PUB WALKS

— IN —

The South Downs

PUB WALKS
IN
The South Downs

Ben Perkins

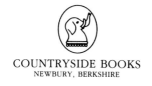

COUNTRYSIDE BOOKS
NEWBURY, BERKSHIRE

First Published 1996
© Ben Perkins 1996

Revised and updated 1998, 2000

COUNTRYSIDE BOOKS
3 Catherine Road
Newbury, Berkshire

ISBN 1 85306 444 0

Designed by Mon Mohan
Cover illustration by Colin Doggett
Photographs and maps by the author

Produced through MRM Associates Ltd., Reading
Typeset by Paragon Typesetters, Newton-le-Willows, Merseyside
Printed in England by J. W. Arrowsmith Ltd., Bristol

Contents

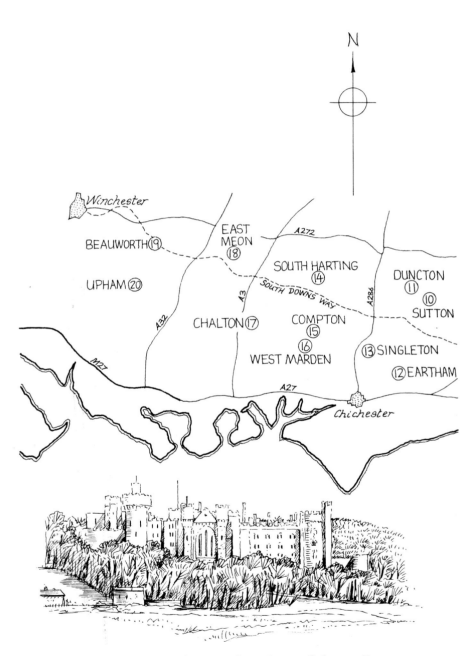

Area map showing locations of the walks.

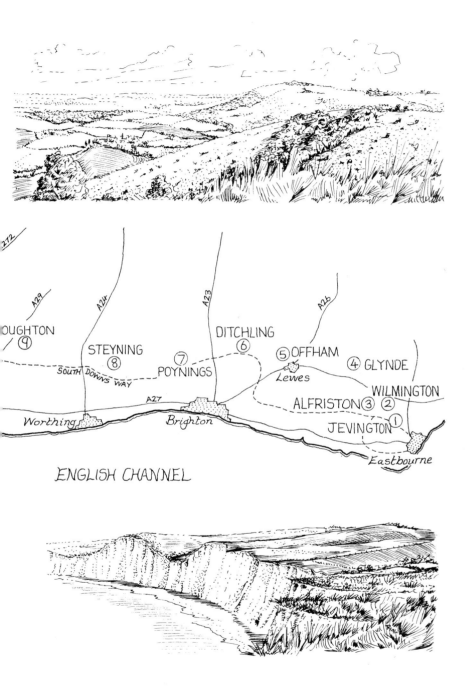

OUGHTON
/ ⑨

A29

A24

STEYNING
⑧

SOUTH DOWNS WAY

⑦
POYNINGS

A23

DITCHLING
⑥

A26

⑤ OFFHAM

Lewes

④ GLYNDE

WILMINGTON

ALFRISTON ③ ②

A27

Worthing

Brighton

JEVINGTON ①

Eastbourne

ENGLISH CHANNEL

Publisher's Note

We hope that you obtain considerable enjoyment from this book; great care has been taken in its preparation. However, changes of landlord and actual closures are sadly not uncommon. Likewise, although at the time of publication all routes followed public rights of way or permitted paths, diversion orders can be made and permissions withdrawn.

We cannot of course be held responsible for such diversion orders and any inaccuracies in the text which result from these or any other changes to the routes, nor any damage which might result from walkers trespassing on private property. However, we are anxious that all details covering the walks and the pubs are kept up to date and would therefore welcome information from readers which would be relevant to future editions.

Introduction

'O bold majestic downs, smooth, fair and lonely;
O still solitude, only matched in the skies'

Robert Bridges wrote these words in the early years of this century and it is gratifying that, although threatened and, in places, encroached upon by the trappings of modern life such as new houses, trunk roads and wireless masts, the South Downs remain much as Bridges saw them.

These gently rounded chalk hills extend for about 80 miles from the high cliffs of Beachy Head above Eastbourne to Winchester in the west and offer some of the finest walking in south-east England.

The most dramatic feature of the downland landscape is the high, open ridge, which is followed by the 100 mile South Downs Way. This long-distance route for walkers and riders offers a succession of panoramic views across the Weald and sections of it are sampled on several of the walks in this book, including those from the Star at Steyning, the Eight Bells at Jevington and the Ship at South Harting. The White Horse at Sutton and the Cricketers at Duncton are well placed for two circuits up and along the more wooded slopes of the West Sussex Downs.

The combes and dry valleys, which cut into the Downs at intervals, are another characteristic feature of this superb landscape. The most remarkable of these, the Devil's Dyke, is explored on the walk from the Royal Oak at Poynings. Another remote valley, recently opened up for public access under the Countryside Stewardship Scheme, is visited on the walk from Alfriston, though this access may not be available beyond 2001.

The rolling dip slope of the Downs is thinly populated and pubs are few. To enjoy this remote and beautiful area where it is most extensive, try the walks from the Coach and Horses at Compton, the Horse and Groom at Singleton or the Victoria at West Marden.

The pubs featured in this book are spread along the entire

9

length of the Downs. I have, for the most part, excluded those which have appeared in companion volumes, so, if your favourite pub is missing, you may find it in one of the series' other books of pub walks in East and West Sussex and Hampshire.

The pubs included are here for several reasons. First and foremost, they provide well-placed starting points for access to the South Downs. Secondly, and just as important, they offer good beer, a wide choice of food and are prepared to welcome walkers, including families with children.

I was agreeably surprised at the warm and positive response which I received at all the pubs featured in this book. Contrary to the popular myth, most landlords do not discourage walkers; and almost all of them are happy for walkers to park their cars in the car park while on the walk (as long as they also patronise the pub, of course!).

Since August 1995, pubs can legally stay open on Sunday afternoons, and I have tried to incorporate up-to-date Sunday opening times for each of the pubs in this book. Some publicans, however, are still uncertain of their future Sunday opening arrangements, preferring to 'play it by ear' until they know how much trade they can expect.

The walks are all circular, between 3 and 5¼ miles in length, and mostly follow clear, well-maintained, paths. Since the Downs rise to over 400 ft, with high points, such as Ditchling Beacon, of more than 800 ft, and the pubs are generally tucked down in the valleys or at the foot of the downland escarpment, you can expect at least one good climb on nearly all of the walks. Luckily, the ascents are often well-graded, following the terraced 'bostal' paths which are such an elegant feature of the northern scarp slope.

For the last few years, practical maintenance work on rights of way within the designated South Downs Area of Outstanding Natural Beauty has been in the hands of the new Sussex Downs Conservation Board, who have done a generally good job on signposting, stiles and gates. The ploughing out of paths across cultivated fields is, however, still a problem, in spite of the stricter requirements of the 1990 Rights of Way Act in respect of the proper reinstatement of such paths – but you are unlikely to encounter any serious hiccups.

The route description and sketch maps should be detailed enough to enable you to complete the walks without referring to an OS map. I would, however, strongly recommend having a map to hand in case you do go astray. You will also find a map useful to get to the start and, while on the walk, to orientate yourself in relation to the surrounding countryside. The Landranger maps should prove quite adequate to supplement the route description and sketch map but if you prefer a larger scale, then the Explorer series, which has replaced the old Pathfinder maps, is ideal.

It has been a great pleasure putting these walks together and sampling the warm hospitality of so many delightful downland pubs. I hope you get as much enjoyment as I have.

Ben Perkins

① **Jevington**
The Eight Bells

The charming and unspoilt village of Jevington nestles in a secluded downland valley, surrounded by hills. The church, half hidden by trees, is notable for its sturdy Saxon tower and flint walls, so typical of many of the churches in the Sussex Downs. The Eight Bells is perfectly situated as a base from which to explore the extensive area of rolling downland between Eastbourne and the Cuckmere river. It is a regular meeting place for ramblers, who are always made welcome and are even provided with plastic bags from a box at the entrance to cover their muddy boots.

The inn was converted from a row of three 600 year old cottages. It has been extended in recent years but remains simple and unspoilt. The bar is divided into two symmetrical areas. One half reflects the age of the pub, with massive oak beams hung with dried hops and a large open fireplace decorated with horse brasses. The other half is modern, bright and airy with windows opening onto a paved patio.

A freehouse, the Eight Bells serves an interesting mix of real ales. Harveys Sussex Bitter, Flowers Original and Adnams Broadside are always available, with an added guest beer during the summer months. The draught cider is Strongbow and Scrumpy Jack. The food menu has been upgraded recently and offers a wide range of dishes. Many opt for the delicious home-baked pies, such as fish, rabbit or chicken and ham. There is also a good choice of vegetarian dishes. The puddings include some pretty solid fare, for example, spotted dick and treacle sponge. Children and dogs are welcome.

The opening hours on Monday to Saturday are from 11 am to 11 pm, and on Sunday from 12 noon to 10.30 pm. Food is served on Monday to Saturday from 12 noon to 3 pm and 6 pm to 9 pm and all day on Sunday.

Telephone: 01323 484442.

How to get there: You can approach Jevington along an unclassified road, either from the north via the A22, just south of Polegate, or from the A259 coast road linking Eastbourne with Seaford, at Friston. The Eight Bells is at the northern end of the village.

Parking: Except at peak times, such as summer weekends, you can leave your car in the pub car park while you walk, but do get prior permission. Alternatively, there is a public car park at the other end of the village, some distance.from the pub but within a few yards of the route of the walk.

Length of the walk: 3¼ miles. OS Maps: Landranger 199 or Explorer 123 (inn GR 562017).

From the front door of the pub you are immediately away from the village and up onto the Downs. A steady climb brings you to the summit of Combe Hill. A ridge walk follows, with wide views over Polegate and Eastbourne and along the coast towards Hastings and beyond. The return route follows part of the South Downs Way.

13

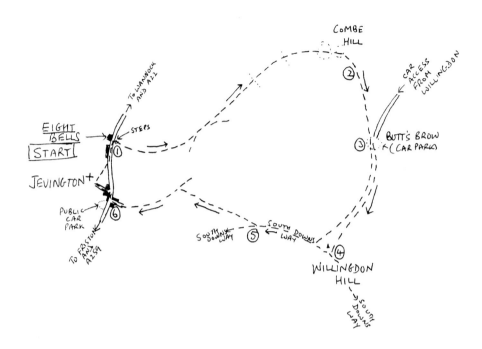

The Walk

1 Start the walk up a flight of steps opposite the pub. A path, fenced at first, then across open ground, climbs steadily up onto the Downs. Where the path divides, keep left up to a stile on the skyline and continue on to reach the summit of Combe Hill, site of a Neolithic, causewayed camp. As you traverse the summit ridge, a view opens out across Polegate to the Weald beyond.

2 The path sweeps round to the right, through a shallow dip and up to a car park on Butt's Brow, which provides an alternative starting point for those walkers who prefer to come across the pub halfway round the walk rather than at the start and finish.

3 Pass to the right of the car park and continue on a clear track where it is pleasanter to sidestep to the left and walk along a broad, green area nearer the edge of the escarpment and offering a series of views across Eastbourne and along the coast towards Hastings and the cliffs at Fairlight.

Walk up to the trig point on Willingdon Hill where the view opens out in all directions. To the south, on the cliff top, you should now be able to pick out the old lighthouse at Belle Tout, between Birling Gap and Beachy Head.

4 Just past the trig point, turn squarely right, passing, on your right, an old stone sign, indicating the direction to 'Eastbourne Old Town'. Carry straight on here, dropping steadily down into the valley, with the village of Jevington in view ahead. You have a choice of parallel tracks and it is best to use the one on the right so as not to miss the next junction.

5 After 450 yards, fork right over two stiles in quick succession and follow a preserved path between two arable areas, soon heading for Jevington church. At the bottom of the hill, with a double gate in front of you, turn left alongside a fence which you should keep close on your right. Follow a clear path through two bridlegates, along the floor of a grassy valley and out to a lane which leads you to the village street at Jevington.

6 Turn right, and immediately left, along Church Lane. Turn right into the churchyard, skirting to the right of the lovely little flint church, parts of which date back to Saxon times. Leave the churchyard through a centrally pivoted tapsell gate and follow a path to rejoin the lane. Bear left for 200 yards or so, back to the Eight Bells.

Wilmington
The Giant's Rest

The Giant's Rest, in this quiet and unspoilt village, has all the attributes of a good walkers' pub. It is a freehouse offering a wide range of beer and substantial portions of home-cooked food served in a spacious bar with wooden floor and tables, unfussy decor and a log fire in winter. A 'touch of class' is provided in the form of regularly changing exhibitions of paintings by local artists. The pub, housed since 1920 in a solid, Edwardian building, was once known as the Black Horse and replaced an earlier hostelry, a few yards further along the village street, now The Old Inn House. The present name was prompted by the proximity of the Long Man of Wilmington, a chalk figure over 200 ft high, which has been carved out of the Downs.

Harveys Best Ale is supplemented by Hopback Summer Lightning and Timothy Taylor Bitter. You can also sample Stowford Press cider and eight different wines by the glass. The food menu varies, but always includes a good selection of interesting dishes such as salmon en croûte, leek, bacon and potato bake, together with vegetarian fare. For your sausage ploughman's, you can choose from at least three varieties of sausage, and the home-made puddings are particularly impressive. An area within the bar has been set aside for both children and non-smokers and dogs are permitted.

The opening hours on Monday to Saturday are from 11 am to 3 pm and 6 pm to 11 pm, and on Sunday from 12 noon to 3 pm and 7 pm to 10.30 pm (all day on summer weekends). Food is served from 12 noon to 2 pm and 7 pm to 9 pm. During the winter the pub is closed on Sunday evenings and all day on Monday.

Telephone: 01323 870207.

How to get there: Wilmington lies to the south of the A27 Lewes to Polegate road and the Giant's Rest is a few yards along the village street, within sight of the main road.

Parking: You may park in the pub car park while you walk, by prior arrangement. There is an alternative car park beyond the church at the far end of the village street.

Length of the walk: 4½ miles. OS Maps: Landranger 199 or Explorer 123 (inn GR 546048).

Starting from the delightful village of Wilmington, the walk follows a stretch of the old coach road at the foot of the Downs escarpment. From Folkington church a steady climb takes you up onto Folkington Hill across an area of downland. The return route passes beneath the feet of the Long Man of Wilmington.

The Walk

1   From the pub car park, turn left and walk out to the junction with the A27, where you should double back to the right. A waypost marks the start of a footpath to Folkington. Cross a patch of grass, passing to the left of a cottage, to find a stile beside a gate. Follow a stiled path through three small fields and then diagonally across a larger field.

2   Beyond a stile in the field corner, turn sharply back to the right across another field, aiming a little to the right of the figure

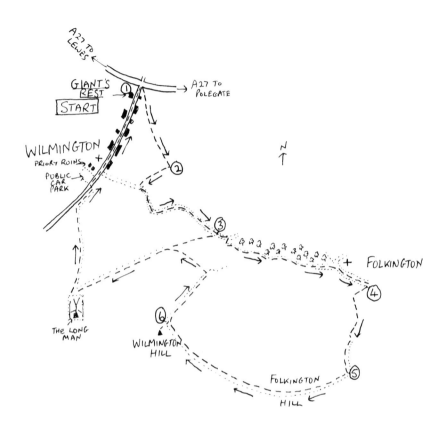

of the Long Man, to find a bridlegate which is out of sight at first over a low rise. Once through the gate, turn left along an enclosed track, part of an old coach road which climbs gently as it winds along the foot of the Downs escarpment.

3 Ignore a path doubling back to the right and continue through woodland. After about 200 yards, turn right through a bridlegate, where there is a notice indicating that you are entering an open access area. Go forward to another notice about soil erosion, where you should go left, downhill, to a stile. Now bear half-left across pasture to join and follow a fence at the edge of a wood. Beyond a stile, continue on a track to a T-junction opposite Folkington church, where you should turn right, back on the old coach road once more. After a little over 200 yards, you will come to a waypost on the right.

4 Turn right along an unfenced path between fields. On reaching a fence corner, bear half-left across a cultivated field, where the path should be marked out. Go over a stile in a dip, where there is another access notice, and then bear right up a grassy slope to another stile. Continue forward.

5 At an isolated waypost, fork right up to a stile on the skyline. Ignore another stile away to your left. Continue to climb, passing to the left of a patch of scrub and joining a fence coming up the hill from the left. Follow this fence up to the top of the hill, with a view of the village of Jevington along the valley to the left. Continue beside the fence, along the edge of the escarpment for ⅔ mile, with a bird's eye view down over your outgoing route to a wide panorama of the Weald beyond.

6 Where a bridlegate on the left provides access up to the summit of Wilmington Hill, you should turn right and drop steeply downhill, with another fence on your left. Follow the fence until you can go left over a stile in it, forward to a second stile and then obliquely down the slope.

Join a track coming from behind on your right, and follow it as far as the foot of the Long Man, where you should turn right through a bridlegate. Follow a path to the road and turn right, back through Wilmington village to the start.

On the way you will be able to look over the wall at the remains of the 11th-century priory, unfortunately no longer open to the public. The church, next door, is worth a visit. Seek out the stained glass window in the north chapel, depicting St Peter surrounded by bees and butterflies. In the churchyard is an ancient yew tree, reputed to be over 1,000 years old. The long village street is lined by many attractive old cottages and is a place to linger.

3 Alfriston
Ye Olde Smugglers Inne

The bustling village of Alfriston, with its attractive village street, lined with pubs, gift shops and cafés, is a popular destination for tourists and coach parties during the summer months, and can get busy. The name of this inn suggests the possibility that it may have been thought up to attract these tourists. However, the sign outside indicates that the pub is also known as the Market Cross Inn. The smuggling connections are authentic enough. Stanton Collins, the landlord during the 18th century, provided a haven for smugglers as well as running a combined pub, butcher's shop and abattoir. The inn was once connected by underground tunnels to other buildings in the village and to the Cuckmere river. The tunnels were sealed, for security reasons, during World War I.

The half-timbered building dates from 1358 and has been carefully altered to accommodate the two main bar areas, retaining much of the timbering and the butcher's hooks let into the ceiling. The ceiling beams are now hung with dried hops and, over the large fireplace, there is an impressive display of old kitchen utensils. At the back of the pub you can enjoy a drink in a walled patio garden or a small conservatory, built against an adjoining cottage and reached up a reconstructed 'devil's step', adorned with cross and coin to stop the Evil One crossing the threshold. The pub is run by a 'free of the tie' lessee and offers Harveys Sussex Bitter, Courage Directors and Pett Progress from the small Old Forge Brewery near Hastings as well as draught Blackthorn cider. A full menu of popular bar snacks and more substantial main dishes including rump steak, gammon and trout are always available at lunchtime on weekdays, while Sunday has a special lunch menu. Walkers who leave their muddy boots outside are given a warm welcome, as are children and dogs if under parental control.

The opening hours on Monday to Saturday are from 11 am to 2.30 pm and 6.30 pm to 11 pm, and on Sunday from 12 noon to 3 pm and 7 pm to 10.30 pm. Food is served every day from 12 noon to 2 pm. Evening meals (main dishes, not snacks) are available from 7.30 pm to 9 pm on Sunday to Friday and from 7 pm to 9 pm on Saturday.

Telephone: 01323 870241.

How to get there: Alfriston can be reached along an unclassified road which heads south from a roundabout on the A27 Lewes to Polegate road, about 9 miles east of Lewes. The pub is in the middle of the village, beside the medieval market cross.

Parking: The pub does not have a car park, but there are two in the vicinity. The one at the northern end of the village is long stay, while the other is for visits of up to three hours. Both tend to fill up quickly during the summer and at weekends, so come early!

Length of the walk: 3¾ miles. OS Maps: Landranger 199 or Explorer 123 (inn GR 520031).

From the village of Alfriston, this walk climbs up onto the Downs to the west of the valley of the Cuckmere river. After a short, high level traverse, with excellent views, it then drops down to wind its way along a remote and peaceful dry valley where public access is now possible for the first time, thanks to the Countryside Stewardship Scheme.

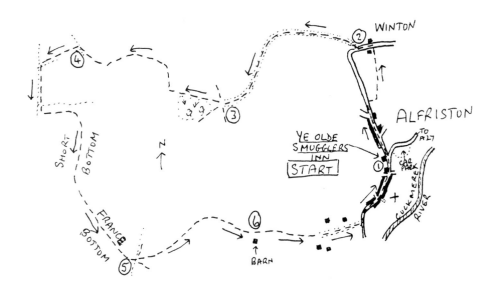

The Walk

1   From the front of the inn, turn left along a narrow lane. At the junction with North Road, go straight ahead and, shortly, turn right on a path, signed as a public footpath to Winton Street. A clear path soon heads north and out to the next lane, where you should turn left.

2   Where the lane turns sharply round to the left, you should go ahead along a broad, roughly metalled track. At the foot of the Downs, bear left with the main track and follow it obliquely up to the top of the hill. Where you have a choice of two parallel tracks, the one on the left gives the better views across to Alfriston.

3   Towards the top of the hill, where five ways meet, take the track directly ahead (in roundabout terms the third exit), which follows the right-hand edge of an area of scrub. Follow this well-waymarked bridleway down into a depression and then, half-right, obliquely up the other side to reach a bridlegate which comes into view on the skyline as you climb.

4   Beyond this gate, go forward with a fence, left, to a second gate. In front of this gate, turn left over a stile. You are now entering a Countryside Stewardship area, to which public access is permitted until September in the year 2002. The views from this point are superb. Over to the right you can see the cliffs above Newhaven, with just a glimpse of the harbour wall. Ahead is the high ground along the coast between Seaford Head and Cuckmere Haven. To the left, Windover Hill is in view across the Cuckmere Valley.

Go ahead with a fence, right, to another stile. Beyond this stile, turn squarely left and follow another fence, now on your left, downhill. After about 200 yards, turn right and drop down into Short Bottom, with a gorse covered slope rising on your right. Cross a stile and follow the floor of the valley as it winds round to the left.

5 Beyond the next stile, where you leave the Countryside Stewardship area, you have a choice of two waymarked paths. Take the left fork, which continues along France Bottom. As you proceed, keep to the left side of the valley, where the footpath runs along a low bank.

6 About 100 yards short of a barn, fork left up steps cut in a scrub-covered slope. A clear path follows the wooded hillside and then descends to join an access drive which you can follow out to the road on the edge of Alfriston. Turn left through the village back to the start, allowing time for a detour to the right to visit the church and thatched clergy house.

Glynde
The Trevor Arms

The neat and tidy village of Glynde nestles beneath the eastern slopes of Mount Caburn and owed much of its early prosperity to one man, John Ellman. Born in 1753, Ellman moved to Glynde at the age of eleven. As well as perfecting the breeding of Southdown sheep, he did much to better the lot of those working for him by building farm cottages and introducing other agricultural improvements. He did, however, resist the idea of a village pub for many years.

The Trevor Arms is part of the Glynde Estate, and the name commemorates the Trevor family, who lived at nearby Glynde Place after 1679. The 4th Lord Trevor was created Viscount Hampden in 1776, and the Hampden family are still in residence there. The pub has been run by a local brewery, Harveys of Lewes, under various leases, since it was built in 1846. Behind the solid and slightly forbidding Victorian exterior lies a warm welcome for walkers – as long as they remove their muddy boots. The accommodation includes a family room, a spacious food bar, and a public bar where dogs are welcome. The windows at the back of the pub overlook a beer garden, backed by the distinctive profile of Mount Caburn. A wide menu of good pub grub is on offer at reasonable prices and may include steak and kidney pie, chicken in the basket and gammon, together with Harveys Sussex Bitter on draught, supplemented by Harveys Old Ale during the winter months. The cider is Gaymer's Olde English.

The opening hours on Monday to Saturday are from 11 am to 11 pm, and on Sunday from 12 noon to 10.30 pm (summer) and 6.30 pm to 11 pm (winter). Food is served from 12 noon to 2 pm every day, and from 7 pm to 9 pm every day except Monday, though this may vary during the Glyndebourne Opera season. Food is only available on winter evening by book in advance.

Telephone: 01273 858208.

How to get there: Glynde is signposted from the A27, about 4 miles east of Lewes. The pub is on the southern outskirts of the village. If you would prefer to use public transport, Glynde station, on the Lewes to Eastbourne line, is only a few yards from the pub.

Parking: You are welcome to park in the pub car park whilst on the walk as long as you also patronise the pub, but let someone know you are there.

Length of the walk: 3 miles. OS Maps: Landranger 198 or Explorer 122 or 123 (inn GR 457085).

This short, but rewarding, walk starts with a stroll along the village street at Glynde. A steady, well-graded climb then leads to the summit of Mount Caburn, the highest point on an outlier of the Downs, with superb views across the valley to the main downland ridge.

The Walk

1 From the pub car park, turn left, cross the railway and walk up the broad village street, passing the village smithy, the church and Glynde Place on your right.

The parish church was designed in Palladian style in 1763 by Sir Thomas Robinson and constructed, using Portland stone, for

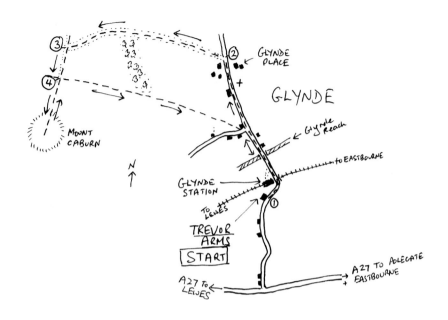

Richard Trevor, bishop, in turn, of St David's and Durham. John Ellman is buried in the churchyard. Glynde Place is a fine, gabled, Elizabethan house, open to the public between May and September on Wednesday, Thursday and Sunday, from 2 pm to 5 pm, also on Easter Sunday and bank holiday Mondays.

2 About 100 yards past the gateway to Glynde Place, turn left through a farm entrance and, immediately, right along a track, signposted as a licensed path to Mount Caburn and therefore not marked on OS maps as a right of way. A broad, unfenced, grassy path climbs gently but steadily up onto the Downs. This becomes a sunken chalky track where there is a well-placed memorial seat with a fine view across the valley.

3 At a junction, just beyond the point where the path levels out and there is a view of Lewes through a gap in the Downs ahead, you should turn left and walk up to the top of Mount Caburn, directly ahead. A notice, en route, indicates that the summit area is a National Nature Reserve. To get the best views, make a circuit of the ramparts and then climb to the summit.

The hill fort was in active use for over 500 years. The original Iron Age ramparts were reinforced as a defence against the

26

Romans who, themselves, occupied the site for a time. From the top you can enjoy a wide view of the main downland escarpment as well as a glimpse of the river Ouse, which meanders close to the foot of Caburn on its way to the sea at Newhaven.

Reverse your steps past the nature reserve notice and carry on for 100 yards to reach a stile in the fence on your left.

4   At this point, turn right, with your back to the stile, and follow an unfenced path downhill across three large fields to reach Ranscombe Lane. Turn left past the village post office and stores. At a road junction, turn right past Glynde station to the pub.

⑤ Offham
The Blacksmith's Arms

Offham is a tiny village, tucked under the Downs on the western side of the valley of the river Ouse. It should not be confused with another Offham, which occupies a similar situation in the Arun valley. According to Judith Glover in her excellent book *The Place Names of Sussex*, the name of the village comes from the old English woh hamm, meaning 'crooked water meadow', presumably after an area alongside a loop of the Ouse which sweeps round under the hill at this point. Behind the pub, the Downs rise steeply, scarred by an extensive area of old chalk quarry workings.

The Blacksmith's Arms was built in 1790 and a blacksmith once occupied the site of a garage, now demolished, which stood next door. A working forge still operates a few yards further along the road, producing a wide variety of ornamental iron work.

The pub is a freehouse and the beer comes from the local Harveys Brewery at Lewes. Best Bitter is on tap at all times with the addition of XXXX Old Ale during the winter months. The cider is Strongbow. The extensive printed menu is changed every three months and there are always added blackboard specials, including some interesting home-made soups. Children over six are allowed inside the pub, but there is no family room. Dogs are excluded from the dining area.

The opening hours on Monday to Saturday are from 11 am to 3 pm and 6.30 pm to 11 pm, and on Sunday from 12 noon to 3 pm (closed Sunday evening). Food is served every day from 12 noon to 2.15 pm and 7 pm to 9 pm.

Telephone: 01273 472971.

How to get there: The village of Offham is about a mile outside Lewes on the A275, the Chailey road. The Blacksmith's Arms is on the west side of the road, almost opposite the church.

Parking: If patronising the pub, you may park in the pub car park, but let someone know before setting out.

Length of the walk: 4½ miles. OS Maps: Landranger 198 or Explorer 122 (inn GR 399122).

After a steady climb through an area of disused quarry workings, this walk crosses a wide expanse of open downland, with fine views all the way, to reach the summit of Blackcap. The return route follows the escarpment edge, up and over Mount Harry. The going is generally easy on well-drained chalk and flint tracks.

The Walk

1   From the pub, turn right along the road. After a few yards, just past the last house on your right, turn right along a chalky track, signed on a waypost as a bridleway to Blackcap. Almost immediately, fork left to a stile, go ahead for a few yards beneath power lines and fork left again on a path which is not marked as a right of way on OS maps but is indicated by a yellow arrow and is licensed by the landowner for public use.

The path climbs between banks, winding through disused quarry workings, now largely grassed over and covered with scattered scrub. It levels out at a large grassy area with the old quarry cliffs rising on your right. From here there is a superb

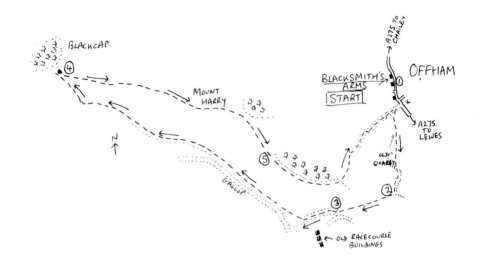

view across Lewes and the Ouse valley to the downland outlier of Caburn.

A clear path goes ahead, climbing through scrub. Beyond a stile, the path reaches open downland. Follow a fence, left, which separates you from the edge of the quarry, and continue for about 150 yards.

2 Go through a gap in the fence ahead and turn right for 20 yards to a bridlegate which provides access to the public open space of Landport Bottom. Go ahead with a fence on your right. Keep beside the fence as it bears right, now on a flinty track.

3 In the field corner, go forward through two bridlegates, ignoring a metalled drive which runs parallel to your route for a few yards on your left. A clear chalk and flint track continues gently uphill. Where it levels out, go ahead through another bridlegate and veer right for a few yards to pick up a post and rail fence on your left.

Follow this fence. Another track joins from behind on the left and you should then go forward along an unfenced, chalky track which soon runs parallel to a gallop on the left, once part of Lewes racecourse. Carry on past a National Trust notice, through a bridlegate and ahead across a fine stretch of open downland, fenced on the left only. After dropping down into a shallow dip, fork right and walk up towards the clump of trees on the top of Blackcap, where you will find a trig point.

The view from here is extensive, taking in a wide expanse of the Weald to the north, the profiles of Mount Caburn and Firle Beacon to the east and a broad downland panorama to the south.

4 From the trig point, reverse your steps for 30 yards only, before forking left along a faint path which follows the edge of the escarpment down into a dip and then up onto the scrub-covered slopes of Mount Harry. Follow a fence, right, over the summit, where, looking back, the trees on Blackcap look uncannily like Chanctonbury Ring before it was virtually destroyed by the Great Gale of 1987.

Follow the fence down to a bridlegate, then go ahead over open pasture and on through scrub. Very shortly, fork right through gorse and across another open area. Go through a gap in a fence and ahead with scrub and woodland sloping down to your left.

5 Beyond a bridlegate, follow a left field edge as it sweeps round the head of a wooded combe. Look out for a waypost which directs you to the left into the wood. Walk through the wood until you can go right through a bridlegate and drop downhill on a chalk and flint track, back to Offham.

⑥ Ditchling
The White Horse

The village of Ditchling, like Alfriston, suffers from its popularity. With virtually no parking restrictions alongside the narrow roads, it can become very busy at times, particularly during the summer months. It is an attractive place with many old houses, one of the finest of which stands next to our chosen pub, and opposite the 13th-century church.

The White Horse was, until a few years ago, a Whitbread's tied pub. It is now a freehouse in private ownership and is a popular local as well as catering for the passing tourist trade. Walkers are made very welcome by the friendly staff. Parts of the building date from the 16th century, though much of it is more recent. The main bar is at the front of the pub while at the rear is a dining area and games room, housed in an extension built to accommodate Canadian service personnel during World War II. Beneath the pub is a cellar dug out of the sandstone ridge on which the village stands. At one time this cellar formed part of a network of tunnels beneath the village, a relic of the smuggling industry. The pub is said to be haunted by the ghost of a robber, apprehended by a previous landlord. There is a 'cold spot' behind the bar and locals recall a horse brass which, inexplicably, flew off the wall and hit the other side of the bar on one occasion.

Beer on draught includes Harveys Sussex Best at all times, supplemented by at least three guest beers, selected from independent brewers such as Adnams, Palmers or Young's. The cider is Scrumpy Jack or Strongbow. The menu provides good value pub fare, including sandwiches and several main courses, four or five different vegetarian dishes, and substantial puddings.

The opening hours on Monday to Saturday are from 11 am to 11 pm, and on Sunday from 12 noon to 10.30 pm. Food is served on Monday to Saturday from 11 am to 2.30 pm and 6 pm to 9.30 pm, and on Sunday from 12 noon to 3 pm all the year round and 7 pm to 9 pm in summer only.

Telephone: 01273 842006.

How to get there: The village of Ditchling is on the B2112 Clayton to Haywards Heath road and the White Horse stands a few yards to the west of the crossroads in the centre of the village.

Parking: The pub has a small car park which you are welcome to use while on the walk. Alternatively, there is a large free car park behind the village hall to the east of the crossroads in the centre of the village. There are also car parks on the route at the bottom and top of Ditchling Beacon, allowing walkers to visit Ditchling and the pub halfway round the circuit.

Length of the walk: 4 miles. OS Maps: Landranger 198 or Explorer 122 (inn GR 325152).

This is a straightforward walk, involving one steep climb, up to the top of Ditchling Beacon (and down again), and including pleasant field paths to and from the village of Ditchling. The views from the summit are some of the best in the county.

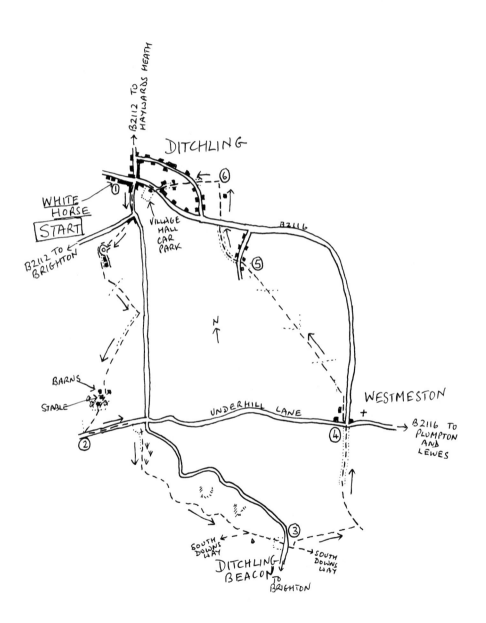

DITCHLING

B2112 TO HAYWARDS HEATH

WHITE HORSE
START

B2112 TO BRIGHTON

VILLAGE HALL CAR PARK

B2116

BARNS

STABLE

UNDERHILL LANE

WESTMESTON

B2116 TO PLUMPTON AND LEWES

N

SOUTH DOWNS WAY

SOUTH DOWNS WAY

DITCHLING BEACON

TO BRIGHTON

34

The Walk

1 From the pub, go right to the crossroads at the centre of the village and turn right again. After about 150 yards, at a road junction, follow a narrow path, signposted to the Downs, which starts between the two roads. Join an estate road at a roundabout for a few yards and then go right between the houses. Beyond a stile, turn left and head for the Downs once more, behind the houses.

Beyond a sleeper bridge, the path, well trodden, crosses a meadow. Ignore a stile giving access to a road on your left, and continue southwards, walking parallel to a fence and stream on your right.

Follow the direction of waymarks, through trees, across an area of mown grass and between two barns. Cross a drive and squeeze to the left of a stable. A path now winds through a copse to a stile and heads across a field to another stile in the far right field corner, giving access to Underhill Lane.

2 Turn left. Just short of a road junction, turn right through a car park to a stile and commence the steady climb up onto Ditchling Beacon on a path within the right-hand edge of scrub.

After about 200 yards, beyond another stile, where you enter a nature reserve, you have a choice of two paths. Both will take you to the top but the one to the left provides the easier ascent. The path winds through an area of old quarry workings and then follows a fine terraced route obliquely up the steep scarp slope, with an expanding view northwards across the Weald.

Towards the top of the hill, bear left along the edge of the steep escarpment, climbing to the trig point on the summit of Ditchling Beacon, at 814 ft one of the highest points on the South Downs. Continue past the National Trust car park to the Ditchling Beacon road.

3 Cross the road and go through the gate, opposite. Go foward for a few yards, past a restored dew pond, and then turn left to a stile. A grassy path bears right to drop steeply down the slope. Towards the bottom of the hill, in another disused chalk quarry, turn sharply back to the left on a sunken, chalky track which brings you down between high banks and out through the buildings at Westmeston Farm to Underhill Lane at its junction with the B2116.

Westmeston church is now a few yards to the right and is

worth a detour. It is much restored, but parts date back to the 14th century.

4 The walk continues beside the B2116 in the Ditchling direction, where there is a segregated path at the top of a bank to the left of the road. Cross a drive, using the steps provided, go over a stile and head out across a meadow to the next stile, within sight. From here to Ditchling the path takes a straight course, well waymarked and punctuated by stiles, or, where it crosses a deer enclosure, high swing gates.

5 At the edge of the village a narrow path squeezes between gardens, crosses an estate road obliquely and continues between houses out to the B2116. Cross this road and go ahead along the left-hand edge of a sports ground, walking behind the cricket pavilion.

6 At the far end of the recreation ground, bear left, skirting to the right of a tennis court. Go through a gate and ahead along a roughly metalled lane. Cross a lane and follow the path, opposite, which brings you out, via another unmade road, to the B2116 once more. Bear right, back to the start.

⑦ Poynings
The Royal Oak Inn

The village of Poynings, tucked in at the foot of the Downs escarpment, is typical of many small settlements which have developed along the so-called spring line, where water bubbles up from beneath the chalk hills, a source of supply which has never dried up, even during the arid summers of 1976 and 1995.

The Royal Oak is a large and busy pub, polular with tourists enjoying a day out from nearby coastal resorts. During the summer months its front wall is almost overwhelmed in a riot of Russian vine and wisteria. The spacious, modernised interior has wood-burning stoves at both ends of the bar, and there is a restaurant extension. Families are made particularly welcome and dogs are allowed if on a lead. There is a large beer garden. A Courage tied house, there are four real ales and draught cider always on offer which are changed regularly.

An extensive menu is available, supplemented in summer by a regular barbecue in the pub garden. Standard dishes include a wide selection of fish, and various home-made specialities.

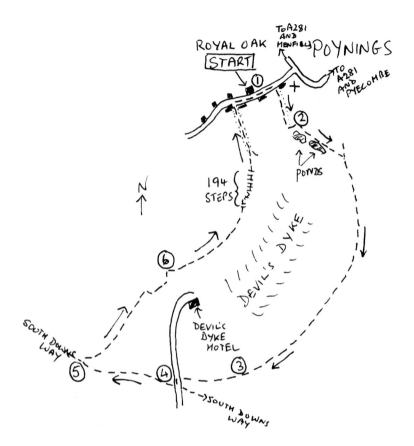

The opening hours are Monday to Saturday from 11 am to 11 pm and Sunday 12 noon to 10.30 pm. Food is served in between 12 noon and 2.30 pm and 6 pm and 9.30 pm from Monday to Friday and between 12 noon and 9.30 pm on Saturdays and Sundays.

Telephone: 01273 857389.

How to get there: The easiest access is from the A281 Pyecombe to Henfield road. Poynings is signposted from a roundabout about a mile west of Pyecombe. The Royal Oak is beside the road in the middle of the village.

Parking: You may park in the Royal Oak car park while on the walk, but let someone in the pub know first.

Length of the walk: 3 miles. OS Maps: Landranger 198 or Explorer 22 (inn GR 262120).

This is a short but spectacular walk, offering a dramatic, albeit well-graded, climb up the side of the deep rift of the Devil's Dyke, and an equally splendid descent of the Downs escarpment.

The Walk

1 From the pub, turn left. After 120 yards, turn right, through the yard of the Forge Garage and ahead along a left field edge. After a little under 200 yards, turn left over a stile, passing to the left of a pond, to cross another stile.

2 Now turn right along the right edge of two fields to join a bridleway and bear right, soon ignoring two signposted paths to the left. Beyond a stile beside a gate, follow a fence, left, gently uphill on a raised bank. As you climb, a dramatic view opens out to your right along the floor of the Devil's Dyke.

A clear path veers right as it climbs obliquely up the side of the Dyke. Where the path divides, keep right on the lower path, still climbing gently. Pause to look back over the view across to Newtimber Hill with a glimpse of the Weald beyond.

3 Towards the top of the hill, ignore a stile and gate on your left and go ahead, now with a fence on our left. The path levels out, with the deep rift of the Dyke still on your right. Down the hill to the right of the path you may be able to spot the remains of the mounting which secured one end of the cable car system that, at one time, straddled the Dyke.

Ignore several stiles in the fence on your left and, where the path divides, keep left, staying close to the fence. Ignore several more stiles in this fence until, finally, at the far end of the Dyke, you can turn left through a bridlegate to join a road.

4 Turn left for a few yards only, before going right through a bridlegate, signposted as the South Downs Way. Walk straight ahead across pasture downland, aiming for the distant wireless masts on Truleigh Hill.

5 After about 500 yards, on reaching a National Trust notice, 'Fulking Escarpment', double back sharply to the right, leaving the South Downs Way and soon following a narrow, fairly level path along the edge of the steep scarp slope of the Downs. The path curves to the left, and passes below the Devil's Dyke Hotel, becoming a broad, grassy terrace from which there is a sweeping view northwards across the Weald and westwards along the line of the Downs to Chanctonbury Ring.

When you are level with the hotel, up the slope to your right, go over a stile in a fence, turn right for 10 yards and then go left on another grassy terrace, which climbs slightly. Shortly, a few yards short of a white-painted post, turn squarely left and drop downhill.

6 After 20 yards, turn right by a wooden waypost and follow a well-engineered path which contours along the side of the escarpment, losing height gradually and crossing the line of what was once another striking engineering achievement, a funicular railway which climbed directly up the hillside. As the gradient steepens, your descent is assisted by a flight of 194 steps. At the bottom of the steps, go forward for a few yards and then fork left along an enclosed path which takes you out to the road at Poynings. Turn right back to the pub, now within sight.

Steyning
The Star Inn

Steyning is not only a delightful and picturesque village with a greater concentration of fine old buildings than almost anywhere in Sussex but it is also a thriving local community. The Star Inn (at one time the Star of Bethlehem) contributes to both these attributes in that the structure is 300 years old and houses a flourishing, award-winning and deservedly popular local. Before it became a pub, the building served as a home for waifs and strays, run by the Quakers, and, according to the publican, still attracts its fair share of them!

The inn is owned by Whitbread and run under licence. It is very much a place for families and young people, but walkers of all ages are made equally welcome. The extended bar is divided into various areas, all with their individual name and character. 'The Workshop' is decorated with farm implements, and the comfortable 'Parlour' is adorned with a collection of walking sticks. Elsewhere you can enjoy a drink in the 'Farmers' Bar' or in a choice of two beer gardens, one reserved for

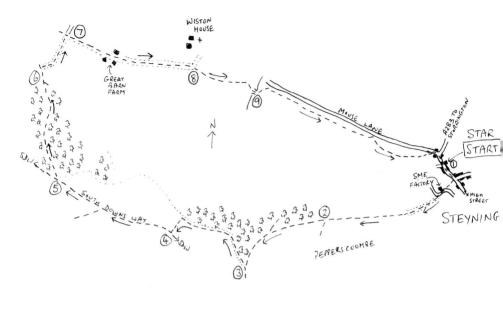

families with children. The real ales on offer, currently the Whitbread-related Boddingtons and Youngs Bitter as well as Wadworth 6X and Fuller's London Pride, are immaculately kept and competitively priced. The cider on offer is Strongbow. The regular pub menu of old favourites is supplemented by blackboard specials, such as curried parsnip soup and pork, apple and cider pie.

The opening hours on Monday to Thursday are from 11 am to 2.30 pm and 5.30 pm to 11 pm, on Friday from 11 am to 3 pm and 5.30 pm to 11 pm, on Saturday from 11 am to 11 pm, and on Sunday from 12 noon to 3.30 pm and 7 pm to 10.30 pm. Food is served every day from 12 noon to 2 pm and 7 pm to 9.30 pm.

Telephone: 01903 813078.

How to get there: Steyning is a substantial village on the A283 road between Shoreham-by-Sea and Storrington. It is sign-posted from the Steyning/Bramber bypass. The Star Inn is on the High Street at the western end of the village.

Parking: The pub car park is too small to accommodate walkers but there are two village car parks which allow you a tour of Steyning en route to the pub.

Length of the walk: 5¼ miles. OS Maps: Landranger 198 or Explorer 121 and 122 (inn GR 174114).

From the village of Steyning, the walk starts with a steady climb along the side of a wooded combe. You are then rewarded by an airy ridge walk along a section of the South Downs Way, with an opportunity to visit Chanctonbury Ring, once a famous landmark but now little more than a battered remnant following the Great Gale of 1987. After a descent through woodland, the return route follows the foot of the Downs back to Steyning.

The Walk

1   From the pub turn left along the High Street. Very shortly, opposite the start of Tanyard Lane on your left, turn right along a tarmac path with a metal handrail down the middle. At the next lane, turn right, veering left and passing to the left of the SME factory.

Where the lane bears right, just past the factory entrance, you should go ahead along a roughly metalled track which soon loses its hard surface and heads for the Downs as a path between hedges, gradually climbing.

2   Ignore a crossing path and continue uphill round the wooded side of Pepperscoombe, with good views back across Steyning and along the line of the Downs to the east, the profiles of Newtimber and Wolstonbury Hills and the masts on Truleigh Hill clearly recognisable. Ignore a bridleway which doubles back to the right and continue up, almost to the top of the combe.

3   Just short of the point where the path finally levels out, you should double back to the right along another signed bridleway, which starts within the edge of woodland, with a large field on your left and the wooded slope dropping away to your right. The path then continues along the top edge of the wood for about 600 yards before turning squarely left and climbing up over the brow of the hill to reach a junction with the South Downs Way.

4   Turn right and follow the South Downs Way on a clear chalk and flint track along the ridge, ignoring a left fork. On a clear day you can enjoy superb views northwards over the Weald and southwards towards the sea.

5   After ½ mile, at a junction where four ways meet, the South Downs Way goes ahead towards Chanctonbury Ring, ½ mile distant – and worth an extra detour if time permits, returning the same way.

The walk continues to the right, on a path which drops down along the side of a wooded hanger on a sunken, chalky track.

6   Towards the bottom of the hill, ignore the first track, which doubles back to the right. After a few more yards, turn right along a clear track which drops down between banks.

7   Just short of the point where the track becomes a metalled lane, turn right along another track, which passes between farm buildings and eventually becomes a metalled drive. Skirt to the right of the grounds of Wiston House, an Elizabethan mansion which can be glimpsed across the wall on your left. It is not open to the public.

8   Where the drive veers left, you should fork right along an unmade track, which continues as a broad, green, headland strip along a left field edge, with the Downs away to your right. In the field corner, go over a stile, bear right for 30 yards, then left to a second stile.

9   Cross a stream and, once out into a field, bear left around the left field edge, soon walking parallel to a lane on your left. You now have a choice of field path or lane, all the way back into Steyning. The path within the field is the preferred option, with much better views. In the last field, you should head straight across the middle, aiming for the church, with the wireless masts on Truleigh Hill in the background.

At the far end of this field, where you have a choice of two stiles, go over the one on the left, drop down a bank and bear left out to Mouse Lane. Turn right for a few yards to join Steyning High Street, within sight of the Star Inn.

Houghton
The George and Dragon

Situated towards the foot of a downland spur, the village of Houghton is well placed, overlooking the water meadows of the Arun valley. Houghton bridge, visited on the extended version of the walk, was reconstructed in 1875 in medieval style. Dating even further back, to the middle of the 13th century, the George and Dragon must be one of the longest established hostelries in the county. The present building, a pleasant mixture of flint and half-timbering, is more recent, but probably hasn't changed a great deal since Charles II stopped there for refreshment in October 1651, en route for France after his defeat at the battle of Worcester. The inn is a freehouse, one of a small chain run by a local company (Surrey Free Inns). The timbered bar area boasts a large open fireplace and the walls are adorned with agricultural implements. An extension at the back overlooks the sloping beer garden, complete with wishing well, and offers a fine view across the water meadows of the Arun valley.

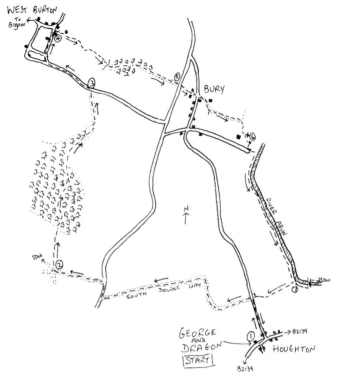

There is a reasonably extensive, moderately priced bar menu. Regular dishes, including lasagne al forno, steak, mushroom and ale pie, and Cumberland sausage, are supplemented by blackboard specials, prepared on the premises, such as mushroom stroganoff, traditional game pie and Houghton pasty. The two 'house' beers on handpump, John Smith's and Courage Directors, are always supplemented by two others, Tetley Bitter and Wadworth 6X, for example. Draught Scrumpy Jack and Strongbow cider are available, as well as locally pressed apple juice. Non-smokers are catered for and children and well-behaved dogs are welcome.

The opening hours on Monday to Saturday are from 11 am to 3 pm and 6 pm to 11 pm, and on Sunday from 12 noon to 3 pm and 7 pm to 10.30 pm. Food is served on Monday to Saturday from 12 noon to 2.30 pm and 6 pm to 9.30 pm (summer), and 12 noon to 2 pm and 7 pm to 9 pm (winter), and on Sunday from 12 noon to 2 pm and 7 pm to 9 pm (all the year round).

Telephone: 01798 831559.

How to get there: Houghton is on the B2139, which links the A283 at Storrington with the A29 at Whiteways Lodge, north of Arundel.

Parking: You are welcome to use the pub car park as long as you let them know and also patronise the pub.

Length of the walk: 5½ miles. OS Maps: Landranger 197 or Explorer 121 (inn GR 017114).

From the pub, the walk soon joins the South Downs Way and follows it westwards on a chalk and flint track which climbs steadily up on to the Downs with widening views back across the Arun valley. After crossing the flat open summit area of Bury Hill a lovely woodland path descends round the side of a sheltered downland combe to reach the small village of West Burton which boasts a number of delightful old flint cottages, several of them thatched. A pleasant field path crosses the gently undulating downland foothills to reach the larger village of Bury where the walk joins the Arun river bank at the site of a former wharf and foot ferry. An easy stroll along the raised river bank brings us back to the start.

The Walk

1 From the pub turn left and, after a little over 100 yards go left again along a lane signposted to Bignor. After another 350 yards turn left along a chalk and flint track, signposted as the South Downs Way. Follow this track as it veers right and subsequently left, rising steadily for almost a mile to join the A29. Cross the road and turn right along the opposite verge for less than 100 yards before going left along another clear track, still with the South Downs Way.

2 After another 350 yards, at a meeting of five ways, where the South Downs Way veers *half* right, you should turn *squarely* right on an unfenced path which heads out across a large field where it should be trodden out through any growing crop. It converges on and passes obliquely through the field boundary to your left and continues in the same direction across the next field, crossing the open summit area of Bury Hill. The path descends gently to cross a track and enter woodland before dropping down more steeply through the wood. On reaching a wider track bear left and follow it down within the right wood edge, ignoring several tracks off to the left.

3   On reaching a lane, turn left and, after about a quarter of a mile, at a road junction, bear right, signposted to Bignor. Ignoring a turning to the left, walk into the tiny village of West Burton which has a remarkable concentration of lovely old cottages.

4   Just past the 16th century Coke's Barn, with its fine Jacobean doorway, on your right, turn right along a wide flint track which continues as a narrower path. Where the enclosed path ends at a gate, bear right with a hedge on your right to a stile and then turn left along a left field edge. In the field corner cross a stile beside a gate and veer half right across a meadow to a plank bridge and stile and on over a second stile into woodland. Follow a clear path through the wood and on along the top of a wooded bank. Where the fenced path ends at a stile go forward along a right field edge to another stile and on between hedges to join the A29.

5   Your next path starts through a wicket gate, almost opposite. Narrow and enclosed at first, it then joins the end of a gravel access drive and follows it out to a lane at Bury. Continue along the metalled drive opposite. Where the drive ends, veer half right along an enclosed path. At a signed path junction bear left, still along a shady enclosed path which eventually opens out to follow a right field edge. From the far corner of the field follow footpath signs right, left and half right past a school to enter Bury churchyard.

6   Leave the churchyard down a flight of steps and go right and left past the site of Bury Wharf and out on to the river bank where the old ferry steps have been recently restored though the ferry itself ceased operation in 1955. Luckily you don't have to cross the river. Turn right and follow the raised right river bank downstream for the best part of a mile.

7   Just before the path and river bend left towards the South Downs Way bridle bridge, you should turn right through a gate and walk squarely away from the river, following a new link in the South Downs Way out to join the lane where you broke away from it near the start of the walk. Turn left and retrace your outgoing route to the start.

⑩ Sutton
The White Horse

Overlooked to the west and south by the heavily wooded slopes of the Downs, the village of Sutton spreads out along a winding village street with no central focus but many fine buildings in a variety of materials, including flint and brick and half-timbering. The church and the medieval priest's house, partly dating back to the 13th century, although not on the walk, can be found at the northern end of the village.

Although only accessible along quiet country lanes, the White Horse, a freehouse in private ownership, is deservedly popular, and can get very busy, particularly at weekends. I can recall a summer Sunday when three separate walking groups converged on the pub at the same time – but all were well looked after. In Arthur Beckett's *The Spirit of the Downs*, this Sussex historian and raconteur describes an occasion when he stopped for a drink at the White Horse in 1909, complaining that he had never heard so much bad language in one short hour. Things have changed, however, and you are unlikely to repeat his

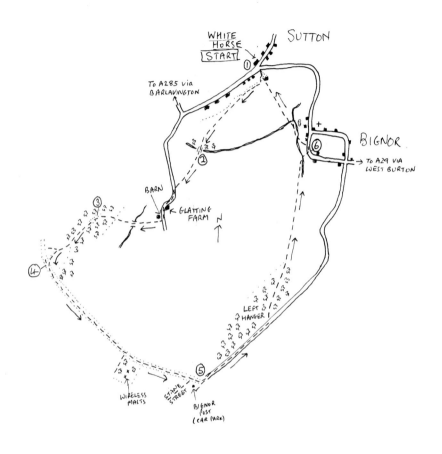

experience. As well as receiving a warm welcome, excellent
food and good beer, you can now stay overnight in comfortable, recently refurbished bedrooms. The premises were built
as an inn in 1746, and the public and saloon bar areas, both with
open fires in winter, lead into a restaurant constructed from the
old wine cellar. In warm weather, you can enjoy a drink on the
sheltered patio or in the secluded beer garden tucked away
behind the pub.

Five draught beers are always available — Courage Best,
Shepherd Neame Spitfire, Youngs Bitter, Morland Old Speckled
Hen and a guest beer. Strongbow cider comes on draught and
there is an extensive wine list. The excellent and interesting food
served in the bar and restaurant can be chosen from a regularly

changing blackboard menu, which can include pub favourites such as beef and Guinness casserole steak and kidney pie, also excellent puddings including treacle tart and lemon meringue pie, as well as some more unusual gourmet dishes. Children are made welcome and dogs are allowed in the public bar. Smoking is discouraged in the restaurant.

The opening hours on Monday to Friday are from 11 am to 2.30 pm and 6 pm to 11 pm, on Saturday from 11 am to 3 pm and 6 pm to 11 pm, and on Sunday from 12 noon to 3.30 pm and 7 pm to 10.30 pm. Food is served on Monday to Friday from 12 noon to 2 pm and 7 pm to 9 pm and on Saturday and Sunday from 12 noon to 2.30 pm and 7 pm to 9 pm.

Telephone: 01798 869221.

How to get there: Sutton can be reach either from the A285 Chichester to Petworth road, south of Duncton, or from the A29 at Bury, south of Pulborough.

Parking: Walkers who also patronise the pub may use the pub car park or the overflow car park a few yards along the road. There is also usually some room to park further along the village street, to the north of the pub. Alternatively, you can park at Bignor Post, on the top of the Downs, halfway round the circuit, and start the walk from there.

Length of the walk: 4¼ miles. OS Maps: Landranger 197 or Explorer 121 (inn GR 979152).

After a steep climb up the wooded northern Downs escarpment, the gradient eases as the ascent continues across open downland up to Bignor Post, which marks the point where the Roman Stane Street crossed the summit of the Downs en route from London to Chichester. On the return leg, a path drops down through more woodland and then follows a tiny downland stream through a sheltered valley.

The Walk

1 Start the walk up a steep drive to a house called The Orchard, almost opposite the pub, immediately forking right along a narrow path, signposted as a public footpath to Bignor.

After about 60 yards, go over a stile and immediately turn right along a field edge, ignoring the path ahead.

Follow a straight course through several fields, with the wooded scarp slope of the Downs spread out over to your left, and then head across a field, aiming directly for the wireless masts on the top of Bignor Hill. The path drops obliquely down through a wooded strip to a tiny brick bridge over a stream.

2 Cross two more fields, still heading for the wireless masts, and join a lane on a bend. Go ahead past Glatting Farm and, just past a barn on the right, turn right on a path across a cultivated field. Go over a culvert, cross another field and enter woodland, to climb fairly steeply along the side of a wooded combe.

3 At a T-junction, turn left, continuing to climb more gently. At the next fork, keep right and, soon after the point where two paths come in from behind on the left and right, fork left and, within a few yards, join a wide, chalky track.

4 Turn left and follow this track steadily on upwards, with an ever widening view across the Weald to your left and ahead along the line of the Downs. At the top, pass to the left of the wireless masts and continue to Bignor Post, where a large sign indicates the route of Stane Street with destinations in Latin.

5 Go through the car park and follow the main motor access road down the hill. After almost ¼ mile, fork left on a sign-posted path which drops down through woodland. Towards the bottom, go obliquely over a crossing track to leave the wood and continue down between fences and then along a right field edge. A short enclosed track, which you have to share with a stream, takes you out to a lane in Bignor.

6 Turn left and, shortly, fork left again through a wicket gate beside a cottage. A delightful path follows a stream along a tiny valley, the only problem being mud after rain. Beyond a stile beside a gate, go ahead, climbing across two fields. For the last few yards you rejoin your outgoing route, out to the lane opposite the White Horse.

Duncton
The Cricketers

Previously the Swan Inn, the Cricketers acquired its present name in 1860 when it was taken over by John Wisden of *Almanack* fame. The pub is also associated with James Dean, who played for Sussex and All England and occupied the pub in the late 19th century. The slim and dapper figure of Dean on one side of the inn sign contrasts with a description of him as a man of extensive girth 'rolling towards the crease like a hedgehog to deliver a deadly straight well pitched ball with a strong curl.' Hillaire Belloc stopped at the Cricketers on his famous journey across Sussex and Bob Copper, in his commentary on Belloc's walk, *In the Footsteps of the Four Men*, recalls the pub in 1950 when the interior was paved with rectangular flagstones. The floor is now carpeted but an ancient open fireplace, with inglenooks and a massive chimney, still occupies one end of the large single bar area.

The Cricketers is a freehouse, offering a choice of Oakham JHB, Archer's Friary Bitter and a guest beer. Dry Blackthorn

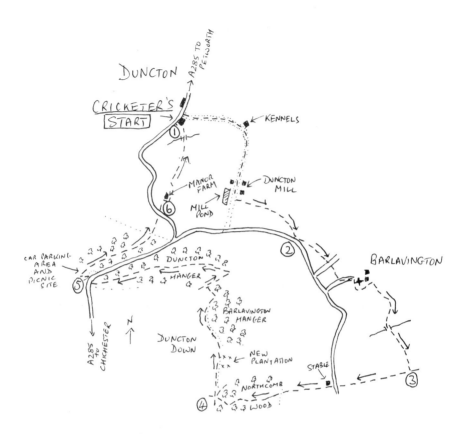

Cider is available on draught. There is a wide range of the usual pub dishes, plus locally reared Duncton Mill trout and daily blackboard specials which are changed regularly. Children are welcome in the restaurant area, down steps behind the main bar. Well-behaved dogs are allowed in the bar. There is a beer garden behind the pub as well as a dog-free family garden with climbing frame, and an old-fashioned skittle alley available to customers and for private parties.

The opening hours on Monday to Saturday are from 11 am to 2.30 pm and 6 pm to 11 pm, and on Sunday from 12 noon to 3 pm and 7 pm to 10.30 pm. Food is served from 12 noon to 2 pm and 6.30 pm to 9.30 pm except Sunday and Monday evenings.

Telephone: 01798 342473.

How to get there: The pub lies set back from the A285 Petworth to Chichester road, on the southern outskirts of Duncton village, 4 miles south of Petworth.

Parking: You can leave your car in the loop of redundant road in front of the pub, or, with prior permission, in the pub car park.

Length of the walk: 5 miles. OS Maps: Landranger 197 or Explorer 121 (inn GR 960170).

The early stages of the walk cross a series of gently undulating downland foothills, bisected by tiny streams arising from the foot of the chalk escarpment. After a short but sharp climb, you will be rewarded by magnificent views from the slopes of Barlavington Down. The return route contours along the side of Duncton Hanger.

The Walk

1   From the pub, turn right along the A285 road for just a few yards before going right again, along a roughly metalled track, signposted as a bridleway. Follow this track eastwards and southwards for over ½ mile to Duncton Mill (private), an attractive collection of cottages and outbuildings beside the mill pond – the source of supply for the trout served at the Cricketers.

Walk between the buildings, noting the remains of the old mill wheel to the left of the path and, just past the mill pond on your right, turn left along a narrow path which climbs between banks at first. Once out into the open, go ahead, ignoring a path to the left.

2   Join a lane and, immediately, leave it again over a stile on the left, diverging to the left of the lane on a preserved field path which then descends to cross a lane and a stream in a secluded dip, and climbs again between banks, passing a massive ancient yew.

Join another lane and bear left along it. Very shortly, go

through a gate into Barlavington churchyard. Walk round behind the 13th-century church, a modest stone building with a simple bell tower. Leave the churchyard through another gate and go ahead, skirting to the right of farm buildings, soon turning right along a wide, grassy path.

Drop down into another tiny valley. Towards the bottom, turn right over a stile and drop down obliquely across pastureland to find another stile and a footbridge. Now climb steeply through a copse to a second stile and then bear left along the left edge of rough pasture, ignoring a signed path to the left.

3 At the top of the rise, cross a stile and, after 10 yards, beside a four-armed signpost, turn right and head for the Downs on an unfenced, grassy strip. Cross a lane and go straight ahead across a field. After two more stiles a path climbs steadily up the wooded scarp slope of the Downs.

About halfway up, go over a crossing track and ahead on a narrower path. Previous walkers have trodden a slightly precarious path round some fallen timber where a little scrambling is required. At another crossing track, bear right up to the top of the wood.

4 Once out into the open, turn right. Ignore an immediate right fork, cross a shallow dip and climb again, up the shoulder of Barlavington Down, with young trees to your right. Towards the top, a well-placed seat provides a good excuse for a rest and an opportunity to look back over an extensive stretch of the South Downs escarpment. On a clear day you can see as far as Wolstonbury Hill, to the north of Brighton.

A track continues through a neck of woodland and then over the flank of Duncton Down, with a wooded slope falling away to the right, before dropping down through the wood.

At a junction of bridleways, go left. At a T-junction, turn right and, at a meeting of five tracks, turn sharply back to the left (in roundabout terms, the first exit). A clear woodland track follows an undulating route along the side of Duncton Down. Ignore a signposted right fork, keeping to the higher track which brings you out to the A285 road opposite a small car park with a wide view ahead across the Weald.

5 Walk into the car park and turn left along a woodland path, parallel to the road at first. At a T-junction, turn sharply back to the right on a path which drops down the hill within a hanger.

At the bottom, cross a field to the A285.

6 Go straight across the road and ahead along a metalled drive for just a few yards before following signs right and left and along a grassy track. Where the track ends, go over a stile, walk round the left edge of a field and, in the same direction, across a second field. Cross a stream and walk up through a copse to join the A259 again, within yards of the pub.

Eartham
12 The George

Eartham is a tiny, unspoilt village on the lower southern slopes of the Downs, only a mile or so north of the busy A27 road but well insulated from it. The much restored church has a Norman chancel arch. Eartham House was once occupied by William Huskisson, politician and MP for Chichester but chiefly remembered as the first fatality of the railway age, killed at the opening of the Manchester and Liverpool railway in 1830. This large, rambling pub dates back to the 17th century, though it has been much extended and altered since. The pub is very much geared to providing food for visitors from the coastal towns, but has not lost the ambience of a good local. You can progress from the plush, carpeted restaurant at one end of the pub to the stone floored public bar and games room at the other.

The George is run by Gale's, the local brewer based at Horndean in Hampshire. As well as their own Best Bitter, HSB and seasonal ales, regularly changed guest beers are always on offer (Eartham Ale, unique to this pub, and the new Gales GB are examples). The draught cider is Strongbow and there is an extensive wine list. The menu is a large one, listed on a multiplicity of blackboards. All the food is freshly prepared and cooked, and includes game pie, steak and ale pie, speciality steaks and a choice of five vegetarian dishes, changed monthly. Children are welcomed. So are dogs, except in the main eating areas. Smoking is not allowed in the restaurant.

The opening hours on Monday to Saturday are from 11 am to 2.30 pm and 6 pm to 11 pm, and on Sunday from 12 noon to 3 pm and 7 pm to 10.30 pm. Food is served from 12 noon to 2 pm and 6.30 pm to 9 pm daily.

Telephone: 01243 814340.

How to get there: Eartham is signposted to the north of the A27 Brighton to Chichester road about 5 miles east of Chichester. After 2 miles along a quiet lane, you will find the pub beside the road junction in the centre of the village.

Parking: You may park in the pub car park while you walk, as long as you obtain prior permission. Towards the end of the walk, you will pass the large Forestry Commission car park at Eartham Wood, which offers an alternative starting point.

Length of the walk: 4½ miles. OS Maps: Landranger 197 or Explorer 121 (inn GR 938094).

This walk explores part of an extensively wooded area of the southern dip slope of the Downs, and provides superb views across the coastal plain to the sea and the Isle of Wight beyond. On the return route, the walk follows an overgrown but well-preserved section of Stane Street, the Roman road which once linked London to Chichester.

The Walk

1 From the pub, turn right, immediately bearing left at a road junction, signposted to Bognor, for about 100 yards. Where the road veers right, go ahead, downhill, on a chalky track. After a little over ¼ mile, where the main track bends sharply round to the left, you should go ahead for 20 yards on a grassy track and then left along a left field edge.

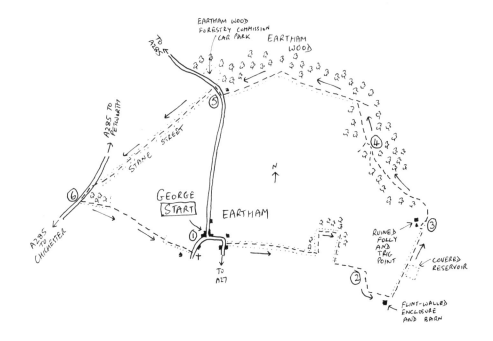

In the field corner, turn squarely right, still along the field edge. At a T-junction with an enclosed bridleway, turn right. After 200 yards, go left over a stile to follow a headland across a shallow dip.

2 At a T-junction with a roughly metalled track, go right, following the track round to the left. Go through a kissing-gate to the left of a flint-walled enclosure and barn. After another 40 yards, turn left over a stile and climb, soon skirting to the left of a covered reservoir.

Keep to the left of two more fields until you can go left over a stile and walk towards a trig point and a ruined folly, built as a summer house but now no more than a shell. Beside the ruin, there is a well-placed seat with a fine view southwards across the coastal plain to the sea and the Isle of Wight.

3 To continue the walk, do not cross the stile providing access to the seat. Instead, turn right and follow a rough track which climbs along the edge of a wood. Beyond a gate, where the main track bears left, you should go ahead on a chalk track through a wood.

4 At a junction beyond a wooden barrier, bear right. Where the track divides, fork right, downhill. Towards the bottom of the hill, at a meeting of four ways, turn left. At the next junction, bear left (almost straight on). After about ½ mile, the track leads out past a forestry centre to join a road.

5 Turn right and, after 50 yards, go left along a narrow path into woodland. You are now following a well-preserved section of Stane Street, the Roman road from London to Chichester. For most of the way, the path runs along the top of the raised Roman *agger*. Follow Stane Street for over ½ mile, out to join the A285 road, where you should turn left.

6 After 200 yards along this busy road, where, luckily, there is a reasonable grass verge, you should turn sharply back to the left on a signposted path. Follow a path through a wood. Beyond a stile, maintain the same direction between trees and up to a stile on the skyline. Follow a trodden path across the summit of Long Down, from where there are good views back and to the right, past the spire of Chichester Cathedral to Chichester Harbour and the Isle of Wight in the background.

On the other side of the hill go through a kissing-gate and ahead on a clear path out to the road at Eartham. Turn left, back to the start.

⑬ Singleton
The Fox and Hounds

Singleton is a pleasant village, built largely in flint, including the church with its fine Saxon tower. Owned at one time by the Duke of Richmond, the Fox and Hounds dates back to the 16th century. It became an ale house in about 1840 and although now in the ownership of the large Enterprise Inns group it has retained all the character of a friendly village local. The pub also has to cater for a regular influx of visitors to the nearby Goodwood racecourse·as well as, in the words of the pub leaflet, providing 'keen walkers with a congenial haven', a statement which I can wholeheartedly confirm. The premises consist of three interconnecting rooms with low-beamed ceilings, two with log fires, and decorated with hunting prints, horse brasses and bunches of dried hops. There is a large sheltered garden at the rear.

The beers on hand pump are Hancocks HB, Courage Best and Bass and the cider is Dry Blackthorn. The food menu is a substantial one, including tempting offerings like beef stew with dumplings, braised shoulder of lamb plus daily specials such as venison sausage casserole. For those with more modest appetites some of the main courses can be halved and there are 'light bites' such as open sandwiches with a choice of toppings (fresh Selsey crab or coronation chicken), a ploughman's style cheese platter or a turkey, ham and pork pie topped with cranberries. Dogs on a lead can come into the bar and children are allowed in the dining area.

The opening hours on Monday to Saturday are from 11.30 am to 3 pm and 6 pm to 11 pm. Sunday opening is from 12 noon to 3 pm and 7 pm to 10.30 pm. Food is served from 12 noon to 2 pm and from 7 pm to 9 pm.

Telephone: 01243 811251.

How to get there: Singleton can be found on the A286 Midhurst to Chichester road, about 5 miles south of Midhurst. The pub is a short distance along a lane to the east of the main road.

Parking: There is a pub car park which you are welcome to use, with prior permission, while on the walk.

Length of the walk: 5 miles. OS Maps: Landranger 197 or Explorer 120 (inn GR 877131).

The walk traverses two low hills at the upper end of the valley of the river Lavant, Hat Hill and Levin Down, both offering superb views. A linking path crosses the southern fringe of the extensive woodland which covers much of the dip slope of the Downs in this part of West Sussex.

The Walk

1 From the pub, turn right and walk out to the A286. Turn left and, shortly, turn right along a gravel track, leaving a post box on your left. After 100 yards or so, fork left through a gap beside a gate and walk along the right-hand edge of the village cricket ground, passing behind the weather-boarded pavilion, to find a stile.

Keep to the right of the next field (the footpath sign is misleading here) until you can go right over a stile and plank bridge over the river Lavant. The stream is often dry during the summer months, but in January 1994 was the source of massive

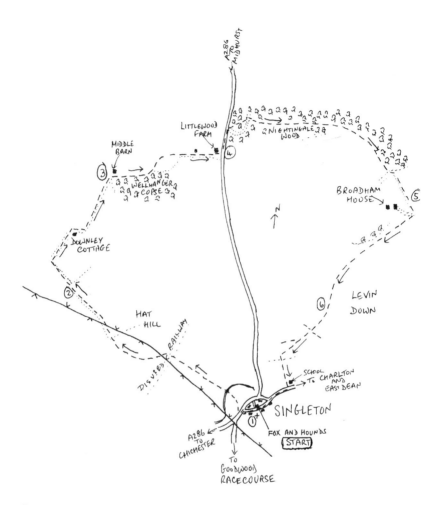

flooding which inundated the village and caused havoc at Chichester, several miles downstream.

Go over another stile and on between fences. Cross a bridge over the disused Midhurst to Chichester railway, go up a flight of concrete steps and continue to climb along the left-hand edge of pasture, up onto the shoulder of Hat Hill. Keep to the left of two more fields, passing and repassing under power lines. A view opens up to the left across to the wireless masts on The Trundle, the buildings of Goodwood racecourse and along the Lavant valley towards Chichester.

2 On reaching the corner of a copse, largely replanted after the Great Gale of 1987, go left over a stile and resume your previous direction along the right-hand edge of two fields, with the copse now on your right. At the end of the second field, go ahead over a stile and turn right along a roughly metalled track which veers left and drops down into a quiet valley.

The track acquires a grassy surface as it skirts to the left of an isolated flint-walled cottage (Downley Cottage). Follow the track to the right behind the cottage, then left along the valley for ¼ mile.

3 The track bears right, leaving a barn to the left and woodland to the right. Follow the track outside the wood, eventually bearing left and right toward the buildings of Littlewood Farm. Walk past the farm to the A286.

4 Turn left along the wide verge beside this busy road. After about 250 yards, turn right into the entrance to Singleton Oilfield, which is, luckily, well hidden in the woods. After a few yards, fork left along a woodland path. Rejoin the metalled drive for a few yards only, bearing left and then turning squarely right along a clear unmade track. Follow this track, ignoring side paths, for over ½ mile to a T-junction where you should bear left down to the buildings of Broadham House, tucked away in another secluded downland valley.

5 Opposite the farm buildings, go through a gate and, immediately, where the track veers right, go ahead up a grassy slope. At the top of the rise, go through a bridlegate beside a solid oak post, the remains of a sign which has had its indicator arms vandalised. Turn right through a gate with a notice 'Boundary of Open Country', and bear half-left up onto Levin Down, aiming a little to the right of the highest point and walking roughly parallel to the trees on your right.

6 Converge on a fence and keep it to your right, across the shoulder of the hill and down to a gate in a crossing fence. Follow an unfenced track, trodden by horses, past a four-arm sign marking a crossing path. About 30 yards short of a gate in the field corner, go left to a stile and down towards Singleton, across a cultivated field and out to a lane between a detached graveyard and the village school on your left.

Turn right and shortly keep left (almost straight on) back to the start. The church can be reached along a narrow lane to the left.

Place of interest nearby

Launched by a group of enthusiasts and opened to the public for the first time in 1970, the main aim of the *Weald and Downland Open Air Museum* has been to save important buildings by dismantling and re-erecting them on the museum site. The first three buildings to be rescued in this way were threatened by the construction of the Bough Beech reservoir, near Chiddingstone in Kent. One of these, and the first to be re-erected at Singleton, is Winkhurst Farm, a medieval timber-framed house. By 1982, over 25 buildings had been re-erected including Pendean, a 16th-century farmhouse, a thatched granary from Littlehampton, the market hall from Titchfield in Hampshire and Lurgashall watermill which now produces over 30 tonnes of flour annually for sale to visitors. As well as buildings, the museum has brought together collections of tools and other artefacts relating to various country crafts and rural industries and provides demonstrations of such skills as charcoal burning as well as special events devoted to activities such as steam threshing and ploughing. The museum occupies part of the West Dean estate and access is from the A286 Chichester to Midhurst road, to the west of Singleton. It is open daily from March to the end of September and on Wednesdays and Sundays during the winter months.

14 South Harting
The Ship

South Harting is a substantial village at the foot of the Downs escarpment, another example of a settlement which, like Poynings, has developed along the spring line. The village supports two pubs. A third, the Coach and Horses, has been converted into a Mexican café.

The Ship was built in the 17th century, using ships' timbers brought up from Emsworth on the coast. In earlier times, the pub was near enough to the sea to provide a refuge for smugglers, complete with a secret passage to the cottage next door. Previous landlords have diversified into teas for cyclists as well as operating a local taxi service. The present owner provides more traditional pub hospitality, in the form of a warm welcome for all travellers, including walkers, though limitations of space mean that families with children are confined to the pleasant little beer garden. Dogs, however, are allowed inside. The pub comprises a basic public bar and a carpeted saloon, where the ships' timbers are much in evidence to support the

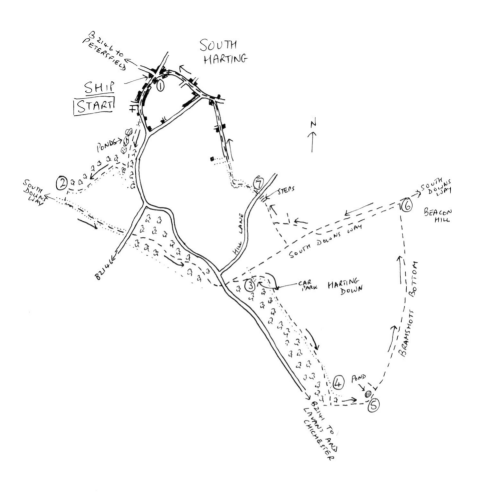

low ceiling. There is a large open fireplace and the walls are decorated with horse brasses and hunting scenes.

The Ship is a freehouse and the real ales on offer include Palmers Best Bitter and regularly changed guest beers. The cider is Blackthorn. there is an extensive menu which clearly distinguishes between the dishes that have been prepared on the premises (most of them) and those that have been bought in. Pastry recipes are a speciality, including game pie and salmon or chicken en croûte. The usual range of bar snacks is available, but only at lunchtime.

The opening hours are from 11 am to 11 pm in summer and in winter on Tuesday to Thursday from 11 am to 3 pm and on Friday to Monday from 11 am to 11 pm. Food is served daily from 12 noon to 2.30 pm and 7 pm to 9.30 pm (except Sunday evenings in winter).
Telephone: 01730 825302.

How to get there: South Harting is on the B2146 road, about 4 miles south of Petersfield. From Chichester, take the A286 Midhurst road, forking left along the B2141, north of Lavant.

Parking: The pub car park is too small to accommodate walkers' cars, but there is usually room to park along the village street while you walk.

Length of the walk: 5 miles. OS Maps: Landranger 197 or Explorer 120 (inn GR 785195).

The walk starts through the village recreation ground, passing a series of landscaped ponds, fed from springs at the foot of the chalk Downs. A steady climb takes you up through woods and out onto Harting Down. Much of the rest of the walk explores this large National Trust area, visiting a beautiful and secluded dry downland valley, Bramshott Bottom. A dramatic descent of the downland escarpment completes the circuit.

The Walk
1   From the pub, walk along the village street, lined by several attractive buildings. Beyond the church and the Café Mexicana, you should fork right along a roughly metalled drive, leaving the café car park on your left.

Go through a gate and ahead, with a recreation ground and a string of well-kept small ponds away to your right. A clear path enters woodland and begins to climb. Ignore the first signed path to the left and, after another 150 yards or so, turn sharply back to the right on a signed path, which, for a few yards, runs parallel to the track you have just used and then turns left, uphill. Shortly, bear right and where the path divides again, keep left, soon walking within the upper edge of woodland, with a fence and field to the left. Continue for 400 yards.

2   Turn left over a stile, then walk up beside a fence to join the South Downs Way and turn left. Now follow the South Downs Way for ¾ mile, crossing, in turn, the B2146 and, after a climb through woodland, the B2141.

Beyond the second road a notice marks the start of the National Trust area of Harting Down, an open space of over 500 acres which we shall be exploring for much of the remainder of the walk. Walk out onto open grassland and ahead, passing about 30 yards to the left of a car parking area.

3   Where you have a choice of two gates in a fence in front of you, go through the one on the right and, immediately, where the main track goes ahead along the edge of the Downs escarpment, you should fork right on an unfenced, grassy path which heads for the left-hand corner of woodland, climbing gently.

On reaching the wood, go ahead, now dropping gradually downhill, with this wood and a fence on your right. After about 700 yards, go over a stile beside a gate on your right and bear left on a path which runs inside the wood, but parallel to the fence and open downland on your left.

4   Beyond a swing gate, go ahead through scrub, ignoring two tracks to the right. At a Y-junction, turn left. After passing between staggered railings, the path bears left and drops down through a thicket, many of the trees being ancient yews.

5   After another set of staggered railings, fork left, passing to the right of an enclosed pond, Immediately past the pond, go ahead, ignoring a grassy track to your left. A similar track now winds along the floor of a secluded dry valley, Bramshott Bottom, climbing gradually.

6   At the far end of the valley, as you approach the edge of the escarpment, you should turn left and climb back up onto Harting Down. You have a choice of two tracks. Use the one on the right, nearest the escarpment edge. Where the path levels out at an open area, a fine view opens up across the Weald with the village of South Harting now in full view.

When the track starts to climb again, fork right on a signposted footpath, which drops obliquely down the scarp slope as a fine terraced track. About two thirds of the way down, ignore the first signposted path to the right. Very soon, at another path junction, bear right and descend to enter woodland over a stile. Go down a flight of steps to a lane.

7 Follow the sunken track opposite for about ½ mile, down to a road, ignoring paths and tracks to right and left. At the road, turn left and walk down into the village of South Harting.

Place of interest nearby

The *Queen Elizabeth Country Park* is easily reached by car from South Harting as well as being accessible from Compton (Walk 15) and West Marden (Walk 16) and Chalton (Walk 17) is within practical walking distance of the southern edge of the park. It is managed by Hampshire County Council, is divided into two parts by the A3 road and encloses a total area of almost 1500 acres. To the north-west of the road, the chalk downland of Butser Hill rises to 888 ft, the highest point on the South Downs. It is crossed by the South Downs Way and offers glorious walking across open pasture. The park area to the south-west of the A3 is entirely afforested. Though severely damaged in the Great Gale of 1987, much of the woodland stood firm. The park centre, signposted from the A3, incorporates a bookshop, cafe and information centre, where you can obtain a detailed map of the whole area with all the paths clearly marked. From here, you can choose to follow a number of waymarked trails, each between 2 and 4 miles in length. Various other leisure activities are catered for, including horse riding, orienteering, grass skiing and hang-gliding; but the area is big enough to absorb them all and even allow the walker some solitude in the depths of the wood or on the open acres of Butser Hill and Ramsdean Down.

15 Compton
The Coach and Horses

Tucked away at the upper end of a long, downland valley and surrounded by hills, the village of Compton provides an ideal starting point for a wide choice of walks in this remote area of the Downs. The pub and village shop face each other across the square which, at times, has an almost French feel about it. It was purpose built and has been in business for 500 years. On one side of the pub you will find a small lounge bar and restaurant, low ceilinged, with some of the original beams still in place. Most walkers, however, will probably head for the completely separate, spacious and welcoming Village Bar on the other side of the pub. Alternatively, when the weather allows, you can sit outside at tables with umbrellas, facing onto the village square, or seek out the sheltered beer garden hidden behind the pub. The former stables next to the garden have been converted into an old-fashioned skittle alley, which can be made available for private parties. Dogs and children are welcome in the Village Bar.

The inn is a freehouse in private ownership. There is usually a choice of five or six real ales, such as Fuller's ESB and Summer Lightning. The good French house wine is available by the glass and Thatcher's cider is supplied on draught. The Village Bar and the restaurant have different menus though a number of dishes are common to both, and dishes from either menu can be served in both areas. The Village Bar menu might include home-made steak and kidney pie or lasagne. The restaurant menu might feature roast quail, duck cassoulet, sliced duck breast in peach sauce, or herb pancake with mushrooms. Both the menus are extensive and all the food is home-cooked, using fresh ingredients.

The opening hours on Monday to Saturday are from 11 am to 2.30 pm and 6 pm to 11 pm, and on Sunday from 12 noon to 3 pm (or later, according to demand) and 7 pm to 10.30 pm. Food is served on Monday to Saturday from 12 noon to 1.45 pm and 7 pm to 9.30 pm, and on Sunday from 12 noon to 2.30 pm and 7 pm to 9.30 pm. The restaurant is closed on Sunday evenings and on Mondays.

Telephone: 01705 631228.

How to get there: Compton is on the B2146 road, about 3 miles south of South Harting. The pub is in the centre of the village, beside the main road.

Parking: The pub does not have a car park but, with luck, you can park in the village square opposite the pub.

Length of the walk: 4¾ miles. OS Maps: Landranger 197 or Explorer 120 (inn GR 776147).

After an easy climb through woodland, much of this walk crosses high, open ground with a series of unfolding views across gentle, undulating downland. On the return route, it passes the tiny, isolated hamlet of Up Marden, no more than a handful of cottages and a tiny, totally unspoilt church.

The Walk

1 To orientate yourself for the start of the walk, stand opposite the pub, with the village shop on your left, and walk

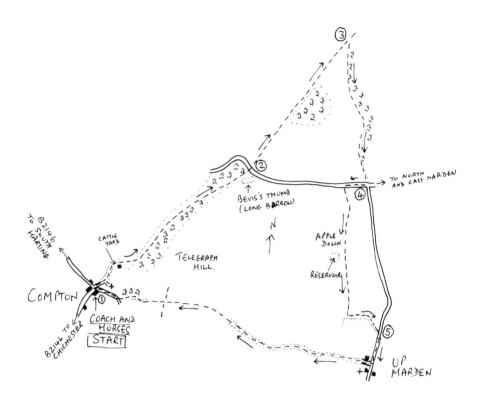

along a narrow lane, signposted to the church. After about 50 yards, fork left along a roughly metalled track, with a flint wall on your left and a barn on your right.

After a little over 100 yards, bear right over a stile, walk through a cattle yard to a second stile and then veer half-right across a field to a stile providing access to woodland. Just inside the wood you will come to a T-junction with a bridleway. Turn left and follow this track for over ½ mile, along the foot of a hanger, obliquely up through the trees and finally along the top edge of the wood to reach a lane.

The grassy mound on your right, next to the lane, is a Neolithic long barrow, known as Bevis's Thumb, and named after a character called Bevis the Giant who, according to legend, ate a whole ox and drank over 100 gallons of beer a week.

2 Go straight across the lane and along the track, opposite, which commands fine views across the valley to the 17th-century mansion at Uppark, now restored by the National Trust after a disastrous fire.

Follow this track for ⅔ mile, ignoring the first signed path to the right. Beyond a stile, beside a gate, follow minor power lines across a field, with a gallop on your left.

3 On the far side of the field, you will come to a stile. Do not cross it. Instead, turn sharply back to the right along a field edge, with a wooded strip on your left. Keep the trees on your left through two large fields, to reach a lane at a junction.

4 Turn right, signposted to Compton. After 160 yards, turn left over two stiles and follow a chalk and flint track up over the shoulder of Apple Down, passing about 150 yards to the left of a covered reservoir on the summit, half hidden by newly planted trees. The path then follows a preserved green strip between two fields and turns left alongside a fence, right, out to a lane.

5 Turn right and, after 250 yards, go right again along the access track to Up Marden church. The unspoilt 13th-century church, reached along a path to the left, is well worth a visit. The interior is simple and atmospheric, with an uneven brick floor and plaster walls.

To complete the walk, carry on along the main track, leaving the church on your left. Drop down into a valley and then climb again, over the flank of Telegraph Hill. After ¾ mile, go over a crossing bridleway, bearing left for a few yards, before descending steeply along a right field edge, with the houses at the edge of Compton now in view ahead.

Towards the bottom of the hill, go right over a stile and drop down through woods. Cross a track, go ahead for a few yards to another stile, then forward for 10 yards before bearing right with a playing field on your left. A track leads back into Compton. Steps on the right provide access to the church, much restored but attractive and beautifully cared for.

16 West Marden
The Victoria Inn

The Mardens are a group of villages tucked away in the remotest part of the Sussex Downs, close to the border with Hampshire. West Marden, only a mile down the road from Compton, is the only one without a church, though it is the biggest of the four. The Victoria Inn has been in business since about the turn of the century. Details of its history are hard to come by but the name of the pub suggests that it may well have been established at about the time of Queen Victoria's jubilee. It is a solid, four-square building which does not look particularly old, although parts of it do, in fact, date back as far as the 16th century. At different times during the past 90 or so years, it has combined the role of pub, shop and post office, but it is now a freehouse in private ownership.

There is a single bar area, with extra tables in alcoves at one end and a restaurant at the other. The draught beers include Courage Directors, Ruddles Best, Wadworth 6X and John Smith's Bitter. The cider is Blackthorn. Children under 14 are not allowed inside the pub but there is a beer garden with a climbing frame, as well as a paved patio in front of the pub. Dogs too, must stay outside. The food, prepared on the premises, comes from a regularly changing blackboard menu, which may include less usual dishes depending on season and the availability of ingredients.

The opening hours on Monday to Saturday are from 11.30 am to 3 pm and 6.30 pm to 11 pm, and on Sunday from 12 noon to 3 pm and 7 pm to 10.30 pm. Food is served from 12 noon to 2 pm and 7 pm to 9 pm.

Telephone: 01705 631330.

How to get there: West Marden is on the B2146 road, about 4 miles south of South Harting. The pub is set back to the west of the main road, a few yards along the village street.

Parking: You may park in the pub car park while on the walk – but please let someone in the pub know.

Length of the walk: 5 miles. OS Maps: Landranger 197 or Explorer 120 (inn GR 772136).

This is a relatively easy walk, with two well-graded ascents. After climbing over Compton Down, with extensive views, the route drops down through woodland into a quiet valley on the West Sussex-Hampshire border, and could be linked with the walk from the Red Lion at Chalton. The circuit returns to West Marden through more woodland.

NB: There have been some recent path alterations which will not appear on older OS maps.

The Walk

1 From the pub, turn right along the village street. After about 250 yards, just before the road veers to the left, you should turn right. The path starts along the entrance drive to a house called Marden Down and continues as a clear path along the side of a wooded slope and then along the lower edge of pasture downland, with a fence and woodland to your right, for 300 yards.

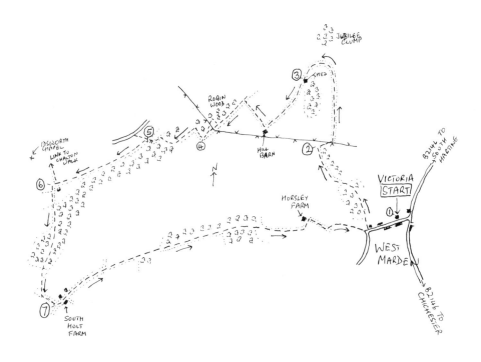

2 Go right over a stile in the fence, forward between fences for 100 yards or so, then left through a double gate. Now follow a clear track gently uphill onto Compton Down, with a clump of trees directly ahead of you on the skyline. Follow this track round to the left across high ground with good views back towards West Marden.

3 In front of a small shed, bear right with the main track. About 100 yards short of power lines, turn right along a headland path, leaving a barn on your left. The track enters woodland. Shortly, at a T-junction, turn left along a wide bridleway. Ignore the first signposted path to the right, pass under power lines and, very soon, bear left along an oblique crossing bridleway.

4 At another T-junction, with the edge of the wood in front of you, turn right within the wood edge. The path soon drops obliquely down through the wood to join a wider track down three steps. Turn left and, after a few yards, break away to the right, down more steps, out into a field and down towards a lane.

5 About 30 yards short of the lane, fork left to follow a fence and a line of newly planted trees. Walk along the valley, keeping to the left of two fields. Over to the right you can see the isolated church at Idsworth, which dates back to the 12th century, though much restored. It contains some exceptional wall paintings.

6 At the end of the second field, where a link path with the walk from Chalton goes off to the right, skirt to the right of a pond, go over a stile and, immediately left over a second stile. Climb, walking parallel to the fence on your left, where a waymark indicates that you are now on part of the Staunton Way. Beyond the next stile, a path continues within the edge of woodland, climbing gradually.

Where the path divides, fork right and follow a track through woodland, partly replanted. At the far end of the wood, cross a stile and bear slightly left across a field. Go over another stile and forward for 30 yards to enter an enclosed track which heads for the buildings at South Holt Farm. Follow this track to a junction with a metalled drive.

7 At this point, the Staunton Way goes off to the right, but our walk continues to the left. Walk between the farmhouse, right, and farm buildings, left. Go straight through the farmyard and ahead on a hedged track.

Where the main track veers left, go ahead along a right field edge and on into woodland. For the next ½ mile, the path takes a straight course through the wood, so ignore all side and crossing tracks. Beyond the wood, continue on a grassy track beside a field for another ¼ mile.

8 Cross a stile and walk along a short, enclosed track, passing to the right of an elaborate barn conversion to reach a junction. Turn right. After 140 yards, go left along a track between banks which drops down to join a road within yards of the point where you left it at the start of the walk. Turn left, back to the pub.

⓱ Chalton
The Red Lion

The unspoilt village of Chalton is little more than a mile to the east of the busy A3 road. Tucked down in a fold of the hills, its tranquillity is marred only slightly by the popularity of the pub, which is easily accessible by road. The Red Lion claims to be Hampshire's oldest hostelry. Built in 1147 to house the builders of the church, it became a pub in 1503. Situated next to the village green and opposite the church, the inn, with its timber-framed walls and thatched roof, provides everybody's idea of a perfect English country pub in a perfect setting. This image is sustained as you walk into the small public bar, which has a large inglenook fireplace and is furnished with simple wooden tables and benches. Move on into the dining area, however, and you might be stepping out of a time capsule. Recent refurbishment has created an ambience designed to meet the needs of the modern pub diner. It is comfortable, spacious and carpeted, with glass doors opening out onto a patio and beer garden with a wonderful downland view in the background.

The pub is owned by the local, independent, Gale's Brewery, based in Horndean, and run under licence. It offers a choice of excellent Gale's beer. HSB, GB and Butser Brew Bitter are always available, supplemented by Winter Brew in winter, plus a regularly changed guest beer, supplied to licensees under the terms of the enterprising Gale's Beer Club. Gale's also offer a wide selection of their English Country Wines, which include such exotic flavours as mead, birch, cowslip or black beer and raisin. The cider is Strongbow. The usual bar snacks are available, as well as an excellent blackboard selection, changed daily. Dishes might include baked rabbit in lemon tarragon or pork escalope with apricot cream. There are always two vegetarian choices. Dogs are allowed in the public bar and children in the dining room, where smoking is not permitted.

The opening hours on Monday to Saturday are from 11 am to 3 pm and 6 pm to 11 pm, and on Sunday from 12 noon to 3 pm and 7 pm to 10.30 pm. Food is served on Monday to Thursday from 12 noon to 2 pm and 6.30 pm to 9 pm, and on Friday and Saturday from 6.30 pm to 9.30 pm; on Sunday from 12 noon to 2.30 pm. There is no food on Sunday evening.

Telephone: 01705 592246.

How to get there: Chalton is signposted from the A3 Portsmouth to London road, about 1 mile north of Horndean and 4 miles south of Petersfield. Follow an unclassified road for about a mile eastwards from the main road.

Parking: The pub car park is small and as it fills up quickly, there is not room to accommoate walkers' cars but there should be space to park alongside the lane in front of the pub.

Length of the walk: 4¼ miles. OS Maps: Landranger 197 or Explorer 120 (inn GR 731160).

The walk starts through Chalton churchyard and continues with a steady climb up onto the summit of Chalton Down, with superb views. A quick descent brings us to the tiny isolated church at Idsworth. Just past the church

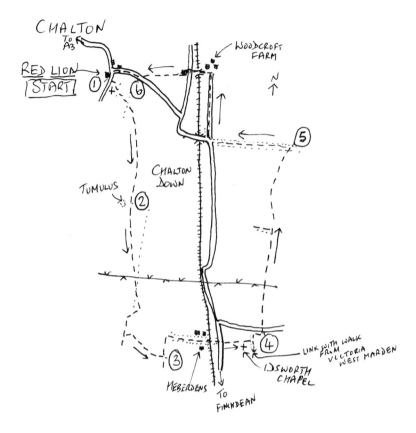

it is possible to link up with the walk from the Victoria Inn in West Marden. After a level section along the valley, there is one more short, sharp climb over the hill and down into Chalton.

The Walk

1   Cross the green in front of the pub and walk through the churchyard, where a notice exhorts you to shut the gate as a sheep is at work. Skirt to the left of the solid 13th-century church and cross a meadow behind it to a stile. A signpost gives you a choice of three footpaths, fanning out across an arable field which covers the whole of Chalton Down. Choose the one on the right, which climbs steadily, marked out by tractor wheels.

2   On the summit of Chalton Down, pass to the left of a tumulus, which has been preserved from the plough, and continue in the same direction, gradually converging on a fence to your left and passing about 20 yards to the right of an electricity pylon, to find the next stile.

Beyond this stile, keep a fence on your right to follow a path which skirts to the left of a battered copse. About 30 yards beyond the end of the wood, turn left along a crossing bridleway which soon drops down, unfenced, between two arable fields.

3 At a T-junction, turn sharply back to the left, soon veering right with the track and dropping down towards a farm. Walk through the farm buildings, cross a railway and a road and continue directly ahead across a sleeper causeway and along a broad, green strip to reach a tiny church, all on its own in the middle of a field.

This is St Hubert's Chapel, built by Earl Godwin, the father of King Harold, in the year 1053. The north wall of the chancel is decorated with some wall paintings, dating from about 1300.

The path skirts to the left of the church enclosure to a stile. Beyond this stile, the path to the right provides a short link with the walk from the Victoria Inn at West Marden. This walk continues to the left, round the left-hand edge of a field to another stile, providing access to a lane.

4 Follow the headland path, opposite, along the left-hand edge of two fields, ignoring a signed path to the left. After ⅔ mile, a stile brings you out onto a roughly metalled track.

5 Turn left, and, at a junction with a lane, turn right along a 'No Through Road'. At Woodcroft Farm, turn left to cross a footbridge over the railway and walk out to a lane. Turn left for just a few yards before going right beside a garden. Beyond a stile, the path climbs obliquely up a steep, grassy slope. At the top, go ahead over two stiles and across a field to join a lane.

6 Turn right and walk down into Chalton. At a road junction, turn left for a few yards, back to the Red Lion.

⟨18⟩ East Meon
Ye Olde George Inn

East Meon, a village of great charm, has to be sought out, tucked away as it is in a secluded valley within a mile of the source of the river Meon. The George Inn enjoys a perfect setting, overlooked by the Norman church and the steep, grassy slope of Park Hill rising up behind it. The river, no more than a quiet stream in these upper reaches, flows by the pub wall as it runs alongside the street.

The George, originally two cottages, dates from the 15th century and has been a pub for 200 years. It is a freehouse, and, during the summer, offers cream teas as well as the traditional pub fare. For ramblers, the owner, uniquely in my experience, provides a leaflet which describes a 5 mile walk, starting and finishing at the pub. I have made sure that the walk described in this book offers a completely different circuit. If you want to make a day of it, you can enjoy the two walks, punctuated by lunch and tea, and, indeed, stay on for the night as the George also does bed and breakfast.

The large bar area is furnished with wooden tables and benches, and there are open fireplaces in the bar and adjacent restaurant. The George is a Hall and Woodhouse pub selling Badger beer of which four are always available on draught, for example, Tanglefoot, Dorset Best, Dorset IPA, plus one guest beer. Blackthorn cider is served and there is a large wine list with a generous variety of country wines, all served by the glass. The food is prepared and cooked on the premises and includes familiar items, always available, such as pies, ploughman's, sandwiches and jacket potatoes, as well as daily blackboard 'specials'. A family room is available and dogs are admitted if well behaved. In the summer you can sit out on a paved terrace in front of the pub.

The opening hours on Monday to Saturday are 11 am to 3 pm and 6 pm to 11 pm, and on Sunday from 12 noon to 3 pm and 7 pm to 10.30 pm. Food is served from 12 noon to 2.30 pm and 7 pm to 9.30 pm on weekdays and from 12 noon to 3 pm and 7 pm to 10 pm on Sundays.

Telephone: 01730 823481.

How to get there: East Meon is signposted to the south of the A272, about 3 miles west of Petersfield, and the George is in the centre of the village.

Parking: You are welcome to use the pub car park while you walk, without prior permission, as long as you also patronise the pub.

Length of the walk: 3¾ miles. OS Maps: Landranger 185 or Explorer 119 (inn GR 678220).

The walk starts with a steep climb and a traverse along the side of Park Hill, providing a fine view across the Meon valley to Butser Hill and the Downs escarpment stretching away eastwards for many miles. The return route drops down into the valley to follow an ancient trackway, full of atmosphere.

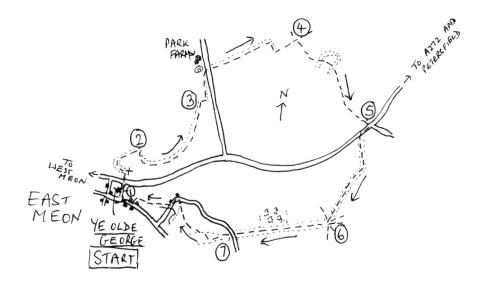

The Walk

1   From the front of the pub, turn left to a road junction and go ahead through a lychgate into the churchyard, opposite. The church, strikingly situated at the foot of a steep slope, is notable for two Norman doorways and for its remarkable font, made at Tournai in France and dating from 1150. The elaborate carving tells the Adam and Eve story.

Pass to the left of the church, bearing left along the back of the churchyard, with a steep bank rising up on your right. An enclosed path then climbs steadily to a stile. Just short of this stile, turn right up a flight of steps and climb steeply up a grassy slope, with the remains of a hedge on your left.

2   In the field corner, with a hunt jump in front of you, turn right and follow a fence, left, along the edge of the hill, with a fine view across the Meon valley to your right. Ahead, there is a good view eastwards along the line of the Downs as far as Chanctonbury Ring, with Butser Hill prominent in the foreground. The path and fence traverse high above a disused quarry and then drop gently down along the side of a combe.

3   In the field corner, turn right down a steep slope for 30 yards and then go left over a stile beside a gate. Go ahead along a field edge, with a lane in a wooded hollow down to your right. After two more stiles you should join this lane by a pond.

Go over the lane and follow the track, opposite, up and across high, open downland, with a fence on your left. In the field corner, follow the track round to the right and, after 30 yards, veer left, still with the track, which drops down into a shallow depression, with a hedge to the left.

4 At the bottom of the dip, at a T-junction, turn right along a clear track. At a Y-junction, go ahead between the branches of the Y, down a steep bank, to join another metalled track.

Follow this track as it drops downhill, with steep slopes rising up on either side and another fine view of Butser Hill, ahead. Towards the bottom of the hill, you have a choice of three tracks. Follow the one in the middle, through a gap to the right of a hunt jump. Follow a well-trodden bridleway, which tends to be muddy after rain, for ¼ mile, out to a road.

5 Turn right and, after about 100 yards, fork left along a track, where there is a notice prohibiting motor vehicles. Where this track bears left to a gate, go ahead between low wooden posts and continue for about ½ mile.

6 When you come to a rather boggy area where no less than six rights of way meet, ignore the first one, which goes back to the right, but go forward for about 50 yards through the trees and then turn squarely right. In roundabout terms this would be the third exit, reading clockwise.

Follow this track due west. It is churned up by horses and motor vehicles in places but there are dry ways round. Cross a track linking two fields. Shortly, join a drive from a private property and follow it out to a lane.

7 Cross the lane and walk up the ramped track, opposite, to a stile. After a few yards, go left over a second stile and diverge from the fence on your left, at the same time converging on a line of spindly trees to your left. Almost as soon as you have met the trees, you should veer right and, where you have a choice of two stiles in a fence, go over the one on the right.

Cross a field towards the buildings of East Meon, aiming for another stile. Do not cross this stile, but, instead, carry on along the left field edge, with the river Meon on your left. In the field corner go over two stiles to join a lane opposite the thatched Bottle Ale Cottages.

Turn left along the lane, past more thatched cottages and an interesting thatched shed. Just short of a bridge over the Meon, turn right, with the stream on your left. The path meanders past some allotments to a junction. Turn left, soon walking under a thatched tunnel between two houses to join a lane. Turn right and follow the Meon through the village to the pub.

19 Beauworth
Milbury's

Situated high on Millbarrow Down at a meeting of several ancient trackways, this inn has served travellers for 300 years. Previously known as the Fox and Hounds, and before that the Hare and Hounds, it is now named after the Bronze Age Millbarrow, which is visible as an earth mound in the nearby field. The rambling, atmospheric interior of the pub was carefully restored in 1963 when a boarded-up attic room was opened up and converted into an area called the Minstrel's Gallery. At the same time, a large inglenook fireplace was revealed after no less than five superimposed fireplaces had been stripped away. Next to the flagstoned bar is the Wheel Room, at one time a kitchen, half-filled with a giant treadmill, once used to draw water from the adjacent 300 ft well, which is now spotlit and covered with a metal grille. At the other end of the pub is a large dining room.

Milbury's is a freehouse and it is a popular staging point for walkers along the South Downs Way, which passes the door.

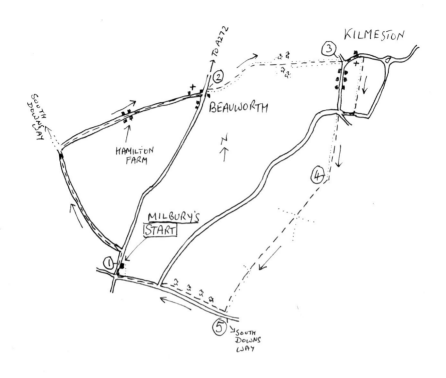

An impressive selection of real ale is always on offer, including Tetley Bitter, Hampshire Brewery's King Alfred and Milbury's own Best Bitter from the Triple FFF brewery in Alton. There is a long wine list and the cider is Blackthorn. The extensive lunch and evening menus which might include beef carbonade, chilli con carne or beef and Guinness pie, are supplemented on Sunday by brunch, when you can choose from a full English breakfast, Scottish kippers or continental-style croissants. Children are welcome in the Wheel Room, Minstrel's Gallery and Skittle Room, and dogs are also permitted.

The opening hours on Monday to Saturday are from 11 am to 3 pm and 6 pm to 11 pm, and on Sunday from 12 noon to 4 pm and 7 pm to 10.30 pm. Food is served daily from 12 noon to 3 pm and 7 pm to 9.30 pm. Brunch is available on Sundays from 9.30 am to 11 am.

Telephone: 01962 771248.

How to get there: Beauworth is signposted from the A272 Winchester to Petersfield road, about 6 miles east of Winchester. Drive through the village and the pub is beside the next crossroads, after a further mile.

Parking: The pub has a large car park and you are welcome to park there while on the walk, but let someone in the pub know first.

Length of the walk: 5 miles. OS Maps: Landranger 185 or Explorer 132 (inn GR 569246).

Starting high on the Downs, the walk crosses gently undulating open downland, about half of the route being on quiet lanes or tracks. It uses sections of two long-distance routes, the South Downs Way and the Wayfarer's Walk, and visits the tiny, unspoilt villages of Beauworth and Kilmeston.

The Walk

1   From the pub, turn right and, shortly, fork left, signposted as the South Downs Way. After just over ½ mile, where the South Downs Way goes ahead, you should bear right, still on a metalled lane, which, thankfully, carries farm traffic only. Pass through the buildings at Hamilton Farm and follow the lane for another ½ mile or so to reach the tiny village of Beauworth. Pass the little church, a Victorian structure with an unusual bell tower, and continue past two attractive thatched cottages to reach a road junction.

2   Turn left and, after 30 yards, go right over a stile and along a right field edge. Ignore a stile on your right. After another 60 yards, go ahead over a second stile and bear left along a left field edge, following a line of trees, many of them gnarled and ancient.

In the field corner, go ahead, over a stile and along a track through a neck of woodland, and on, between hedges, for ¼ mile or so to reach a road junction at Kilmeston.

3   Follow the road, opposite, past the church, a simple structure with a weather-boarded bell tower. After another 50 yards or so, turn right on a signposted path, part of the Wayfarer's Walk, a 70 mile long-distance path linking Inkpen

Beacon in Berkshire with Emsworth on the Channel coast.

Once out into a field, follow a bank and then a hedge to the next stile and, after three more stiles, follow a pleasant path within a wooded strip out to a lane. Turn right and, at a road junction, go over the stile in front of you. Follow the footpath signs across a paddock to a stile near the far right-hand field corner and then cross three more fields, walking parallel to the right field edge, with stiles at all the intermediate boundaries.

4 In the fourth field, go forward for 50 yards before going right over a stile. Turn left and, immediately, bear right, diverging from the hedge on your left at an angle of about 40 degrees to cross a vast prairie field. Although it has been ploughed and planted, the path is normally marked out by tyre marks and previous walkers. Go through a gap to the right of a prominent tree and maintain your direction across another big field.

On the other side of this field, cross a stile and climb along the left-hand edge of parkland, with a fence on your left. At the top of the slope, pause to look back over a wide, panoramic view to the north.

5 Cross a stile and turn right along a track which runs within the trees, parallel and to the right of a lane. You are now back on the South Downs Way. At a road junction, go ahead beside the road for 300 yards before turning right into the pub's car park.

⓴ Upham
The Brushmakers Arms

Although within easy reach of Winchester and Southampton, the peaceful village of Upham remains quiet and totally unspoilt. The building which now houses the Brushmakers Arms is 600 years old. Before becoming a pub it was, at different times, a school and a centre for itinerant brushmakers, who toured the country selling brooms and brushes manufactured from hazel, cut from local hedges. In 1644 the premises briefly became Oliver Cromwell's campaign headquarters. In more recent times, when threatened with conversion to a restaurant, the Brushmakers Arms was purchased by a group of villagers and is now a rented freehouse. It is, reputedly, visited at intervals by the spirit of a miserly brushmaker who was murdered for his money about 400 years ago.

The cosy, low-ceilinged bar is separated into two areas by a central chimney and log-burning stove, and is comfortably furnished following discreet extension and modernisation. The decor is supplemented, appropriately enough, by a variety of

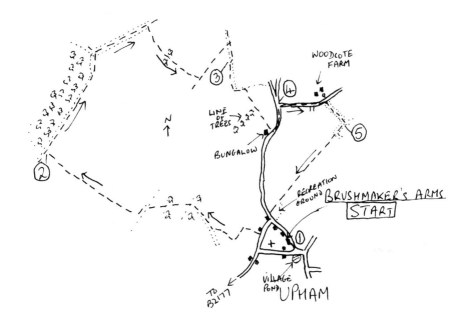

broom and brushes. The real ales, always available, are Ringwood Best Bitter, Draught Bass and the pub's own Brush Best Bitter, in addition to a regularly changed guest beer. The ciders are Strongbow and Addlestone's. The pub offers separate lunch and evening menus. At lunchtime, when most walkers are about, you can choose from six different ploughman's, ten types of jacket potato and assorted sandwiches, or hot croissants, with interesting fillings such as bacon and Stilton, as well as a variety of more substantial dishes and home-made blackboard specials. Families are made welcome and dogs are not excluded. Smoking is allowed. Outside, there is a terrace and a beer garden.

The opening hours on Monday to Thursday are from 11 am to 2.30 pm and 5.30 pm to 11 pm, on Friday and Saturday from 11 am to 3 pm and 5.30 pm to 11 pm and on Sunday from 12 noon to 3.30 pm and 7 pm to 10.30 pm. Food is served every day from 12 noon to 2 pm and 7 pm to 9.30 pm.

Telephone: 01489 860231.

How to get there: The village of Upham is signposted to the north of the B2177 Winchester to Bishop's Waltham road. To

94

find the pub, drive either way round the triangle of roads at the centre of the village.

Parking: The pub does not have a car park, but there is room to park nearby, beside the village pond.

Length of the walk: 4½ miles. OS Maps: Landranger 185 or Explorer 119 or 132 (inn GR 540206).

This walk crosses open, mainly arable, downland at the south-western corner of the South Downs. It offers easy walking, mostly on clear tracks. The final section, along a ridge, offers excellent views across miles of rolling downland.

The Walk

1 From the pub, turn right and, at a T-junction, go right again. Walk past the church and, at another junction, fork right once more. After 100 yards or so, go left through a gate and diverge slightly from the fence on your right to a stile, which is within sight. Beyond this stile, follow the left-hand edge of a field round, joining a track which comes in from behind on your left. Go ahead, still along the left field edge and, in the field corner, go ahead on a woodland track, soon ignoring a right fork.

A trodden path drops down into a shallow valley, passes through a wooded strip and climbs again, without changing direction, to another stile, within sight. Beyond this stile, go left along the field edge and then right along a clear, unplanted track across the middle of a large, cultivated field. Continue for ½ mile.

2 At the edge of a wood, turn right along a clear track. After another ¼ mile, follow the main track as it veers right, away from the wood, between fields. After a further ¼ mile, turn right over a stile and follow a left field edge.

In the field corner, go ahead through a belt of woodland and on beside another field. In the next field corner, after a short, steep climb, fork left, soon between fence and hedge. Cross a gallop, go through a gap in the hedge and turn right on a track, also used by horses.

3 Now take care as it is easy to go wrong. Where the track curves to the left, bear right through a gap in the hedge on your right and then drop downhill with this hedge on your left. Soon after the hedge veers left, your path breaks away to the right across a cultivated field where there may be no visible path through the crop. Aim to pass to the left of a peninsula of scrub protruding into the field from the right and then drop down across a field to join a lane to the left of a bungalow. Turn left and continue for 200 yards.

4 Turn right, signposted to Woodcote. Walk past Woodcote Farm on the left and, shortly, fork right on a rough track, labelled as part of an off road cycle route.

5 Soon after the point where the track levels out and starts to drop down, fork right along another track, signposted as a footpath only. It soon bears right and climbs. Ignore a path and track to the left and go straight ahead, up and along an airy ridge, offering the best views on the walk.

Follow this path back to Upham, finally passing to the right of a sports field to join a lane at a junction. Turn left, signposted to Bishop's Waltham, and within a few minutes, you will be back at the pub.